3

599 Dob

MAMMALS

Text by Luděk J. Dobroruka

Illustrations by Zdeněk Berger

BLITZ EDITIONS

Text by Luděk J. Dobroruka
Translated by Marie Hejlová
Illustrations by Zdeněk Berger
Graphic design by Antonín Chmel

Designed and produced by Aventinum Publishing House,
Prague, Czech Republic
This English edition published 1998 by Blitz Editions,
an imprint of Bookmart Ltd.
Registered Number 2372865
Trading as Bookmart Limited
Desford Road, Enderby, Leicester LE9 5AD

ISBN 1-85605-446-2
Printed in the Czech Republic by Polygrafia, a.s., Prague
3/07/17/51-02

Contents

Characteristics of mammals   6

Where mammals live   7

Developmental adaptation in mammals   9
    Movement   9
    Feeding   13
    Fur, horns and antlers   16

Behaviour   18

Communication   20

Mammalian communities   25

Mammalian tracks and traces   26

How to observe and study mammals   28

How to measure mammals   31

Key for the identification of orders
    and families of European mammals   33

Plates   40

Index   185

Bibliography   190

Characteristics of mammals

Mammals are only a small part of the whole living kingdom. Zoologists recognize between 3 and 10 million living species of animals. (The wide range in total estimates of different species reflects differences in opinion over whether a particular animal can be considered as a distinct species or as a subspecies.) The arthropods (phylum Arthropoda) comprise the largest number of present-day species, the insects alone amounting to more than 1.6 million. Even so, entomologists reckon that only a tenth or so of all insect species have as yet been discovered and described. The molluscs (phylum Mollusca) are also very numerous, comprising around 50,000 species. In comparison there are only about 8,600 species of birds (Aves) and some 5,000 of mammals (Mammalia).

Mammals are the most developmentally advanced group of vertebrates. They can be simply and unambiguously distinguished from other vertebrates by two features which appear nowhere else in the animal kingdom. They are wholly or partially covered with fur or hair, and they feed their young with milk produced in the mother's mammary glands—from which they take their name. Only the most primitive mammals (the Prototheria) lay eggs, in all other mammals (the Eutheria) the embryo develops within the mother's body, in the womb, nourished through the placenta, and is born in various stages of development. All mammals are suckled on their mother's milk after they are born.

One of the most obvious characteristics of mammals is that they are 'warm blooded' — they maintain a constant body temperature within a wide range of external conditions (a feature they share with birds) and have a relatively high metabolic rate.

As a class they possess various features of body organization and internal structure in common. Anatomical features that distinguish mammals are the possession of a simple lower jaw attached to the skull by a secondary maxillary joint on the temporal bone (see fig. 6), a constant number (7) of vertebrae in the neck, three ossicles in the middle ear, and differentiated teeth. Visible external ears (auricles) are also a common mammalian characteristic. The thoracic and abdominal cavities are separated by a powerful flat circular muscle, the diaphragm, which is involved in breathing. The heart is divided into four chambers, two atria (sing. atrium) and two ventricles, which allows a complete separation of the pulmonary (lung-heart) blood circulatory system from that of the rest of the body. In all mammals the aorta (the main artery leaving the heart) forms a single leftward arch. Mature mammalian red blood cells can be distinguished from those of birds by their lack of a cell nucleus.

Mammals have highly developed brains, particularly the secondary cortex of the forebrain, which in the most advanced species is intricately convoluted and lobed. A characteristic of mammalian brains is the pons, which includes connecting links between the forebrain and the cerebellum.

In some species or groups of species, certain typical mammalian characteristics have of course become modified. Seals typically lack external ears, whales and dolphins (cetaceans) are not covered in fur, toothed cetaceans have uniformly shaped teeth, the metabolism of hibernating animals varies in response to the outside environment, and so on.

In appearance mammals are enormously diverse. Some are no more than a few centimetres long, and weigh only a gram or so, the great whales on the other hand can reach 30 metres long and weigh 150 tonnes. Mammals' ability to regulate their body temperature to a constant 36-39 °C has enabled them to colonize the most extreme environments, from the heat of the deserts to the deadly chill of the polar regions.

As with any class of animals there are differences of opinion over the classification of various mammals as species or subspecies, geographic races and so on. The minutiae of these arguments, important though they may be for studies of differentiation and evolution of species will not concern us here. Some zoologists, for example, believe the recognizably different European Wild Cat and the African Wild Cat to be two distinct species; others consider them to be only different subspecies of the same species. However they all agree that *Felis silvestris* and *Felis lybica* (respectively the European and African Wild Cat) belong to the genus *Felis*, of the family Felidae, of the order Carnivora and belong to the class Mammalia. These categories are quite sufficient for our requirements. For those interested in wild-life, it is more important to be able to know how to distinguish the African from the European Wild Cat, than to determine whether they are independent species.

Where mammals live

The distribution of plant and animal species is determined by many different factors, amongst which climate and geography are of overriding importance. The land surface of the globe can be divided into large geographic regions separated from each other by almost insurmountable climatic and topographic barriers such as deserts and oceans. The English naturalist Alfred Russel Wallace first delimited six such regions, each with its characteristic indigenous fauna and flora, in 1876. The European and Mediterranean area with which we are concerned forms part of the Palearctic zoogeographic region which, roughly speaking, includes all the non-tropical parts of Europe, Asia and Africa.

Within a main geographic region there are of course many different kinds of habitat—grassland, forests, lakes, mountains, seas—which are determined primarily by climate and terrain, and are also defined in terms of the characteristic plants and animals present within them. These habitat categories are known as *biomes*. Terrestrial biomes comprise many different types of communities and range from virgin forest to the cold, treeless tundra, and from tropical rain forests to semi-deserts and deserts.

Each biome comprises many smaller communities in which each species has its *niche*. The idea of a niche encompasses the function of an animal or plant within a community and its relation to the other members of the community, which for animals means primarily where they live and what they eat. As a rule, animals develop ways of exploiting their niche to the utmost. Every niche is characterized by a vast range of subtle differences which are all the more relevant to the organism the smaller it is. Some animal species are very adaptable. They are not confined to a single niche and can even adjust themselves to human interference by exploiting the new possibilities. At the other extreme are species whose niche is strictly defined within very narrow limits. They are consequently far less numerous to begin with, are extremely sensitive to any interference with their habitat and tend to disappear from areas which come under cultivation. Human activity is therefore an increasingly important factor in determining the occurrence and abundance of animal species. Man's activities have in most places encroached on the original habitats. Forests have been felled and turned into fields, deserts have been fertilized and irrigated, wetlands have been drained.

When we come to consider the distribution of individual animals rather than species, there are many more factors to be considered. Individual animals do not usually range over the whole of their potential habitat at random but have a more or less restricted 'home range' in which they live. Home ranges vary in size not only according to species but also with sex (males usually have a larger home range than females), food supply, and the immediate terrain. Home ranges of individual animals of the same species may overlap. Some animals live their entire lives in a restricted area, for others the home range covers a vast area within which the animal makes seasonal migrations (e.g. the seasonal migrations of reindeer from winter to summer pastures, and the migrations of seals to gather in large breeding colonies).

In territorial species, the males in particular defend part of their home range against other males of the species, usually in the mating season, rarely outside it. Territories are usually quite small, often covering no more than a dozen square metres, commonly even less. Animals mark their territories by scent (urine in dogs) or sound (roaring in Red Deer stags), or less frequently by visual signals such as adopting a typical posture, or by combinations of olfactory, acoustic and visual signals.

One cause of the reduction in range for many large mammals in particular is hunting by man. Together with the loss of habitat this has led to the disappearance of many species locally and brought some close to the verge of complete extinction. Most threatened have been and still are the larger carnivores and ungulates, whales, and some of the smaller mammals hunted for their fur. On the other hand, man has, accidentally or deliberately, introduced some species to areas where they do not naturally occur. Some of these attempts ended in failure, some have been disastrously successful (the introduction of rabbits to Australia), and some have resulted in the gradual build-up of a prospering population. Animals introduced into Europe include the Muskrat, the Canadian Beaver, the Coypu or Nutria, the American Mink, the Raccoon Dog and the Raccoon. Mice and rats also follow man wherever he goes. Occasionally, mammals kept in captivity have escaped and built up feral (wild) populations. In England for example we have the Chinese Muntjac, the Chinese Water Deer and the Red-necked Wallaby.

Within any wild population of a species there is a large amount of genetic variability. Individuals are not absolutely identical, and genetic characteristics become reshuffled during inheritance. Individuals endowed with some hereditary quality which has proved advantageous in their particular environment prosper more than those lacking it. Consequently the population inhabiting a particular area is subject to change through natural selection and becomes increasingly adapted to the environment. If the species ranges over a very wide area where different living conditions occur it often becomes differentiated into local populations, easily distinguishable from each other, yet capable of successful interbreeding. Such populations are regarded as subspecies or geographic races, as they usually occur when the populations are geographically separated from each other. The most common visible differences are in colour and size. With a few exceptions, the geographic variability of the species described in this book is not mentioned. The illustrations show the most common colours and the dimensions given cover the entire range of variation.

Developmental adaptation in mammals

Movement

Mammals have become adapted to all types of environment. Movement under different conditions has led to specialization of their limbs in many different ways.

The archetypal mammalian limb ends in five digits (fig. 1). In response to different ways of life and environments these five digits have become modified in various ways, into fingers, toes, hoofs and flippers. In some cases the number of digits has been reduced. An extreme example is a horse's hoof. All the toes except the third toe have disappeared. The single remaining toe is armed with a hard horny hoof, which represents the optimal adaptation for rapid movement on the hard ground of the steppes. Horses are members of the odd-toed ungulates, and ungulates (hoofed mammals) in general provide good examples of adaptation to the environment.

Hoofed mammals can be divided into two groups, the *perissodactyls* (odd-toed ungulates) and the *artiodactyls* (even-toed ungulates). The two

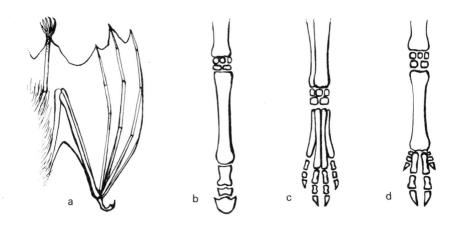

Fig. 1. Various modifications of the five-toed foot in mammals: **a**, chiropterans (elongated phalanges and metacarpals); **b**, odd-toed ungulates (limb axis passing through the third digit); **c**, even-toed ungulates (limb axis passing between the third and the fourth digit) —the animal walks with all its toes touching the ground; **d**, even-toed ungulates—the animal walks on its third and fourth toes only.

groups are not closely related and the structure of their limbs is quite different. In odd-toed ungulates, the limb axis passes through the third toe, which is the strongest. The first toe is always missing, and the number of toes preserved on the forefoot is four, three or one, and on the hindfoot three or one, depending on species. Tapirs, which live on soft, swampy ground, have preserved the larger number of toes to serve as a more effective support, compared to the equines noted above. In even-toed ungulates, the axis of both the fore and hindlimbs passes between the powerfully developed third and fourth toes which each form a small hoof (the typical cloven hoof). The second and fifth toes may be located behind and may form small hoofs (cleaves) which may or may not touch the ground. The first toe is always missing. Hippopotamuses and pigs, for example, walk on all four toes (fig. 1c); in deer, the second and fifth toes, though developed, do not touch the ground in normal walking conditions (fig. 1d) (these stunted toes are called dew claws). In giraffes, pronghorn antelopes and camels for example, the hind toes have disappeared and only the third and fourth toes are present.

In a great many mammalian species the full five toes are retained on the forelimbs whereas the number of toes on the hindlimbs is often reduced. Mammals as a whole can be divided into several categories according to their mode of walking. We can distinguish *plantigrade* mammals (e.g. bears, fig. 2a) which walk on the entire sole of the foot and those that walk on only the front part of the sole (e.g. Genet, Ichneumon); *digitigrade* mammals which walk on their toes (e.g. dogs, cats, fig. 2b); and *unguli-grades*, only whose toe tips touch the ground (the ungulates, fig. 2c). The

Fig. 2. Ways of walking: **a**, with the entire sole of the foot on the ground; **b**, on the toes; **c**, on the tips of the toes; **d**, analagous position in man.

last segment of each toe usually bears some form of horny structure, either claws, nails (in higher primates) or hoofs.

The most common gait in mammals is the alternate step in which a forelimb and the opposite hindlimb move forward together. Animals of open spaces such as the steppes and deserts have very often developed a gait in which both legs on the same side of the body move forward together. This produces the characteristic ambling gait of camels. Most mammals walk on four legs but some are at least intermittently bipedal, that is they move around on two (hind) limbs. This mode of locomotion reaches its highest degree of adaptation in man, but there are other mammals that, although making use of all four limbs to move around slowly, run or jump on powerful and elongated hindlimbs when moving rapidly. Kangaroos and wallabies are the best known example but jerboas and desert rats also move in this way.

The forelimbs of moles have become adapted to their underground life. They have completely lost the ability to support the animal in the usual fashion when walking and have developed into spatulate structures that

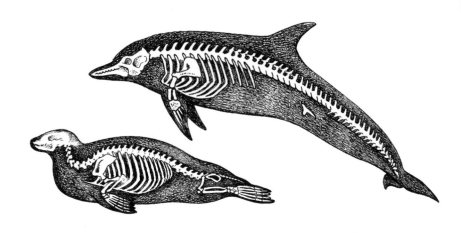

Fig. 3. Skeleton of a seal.

Fig. 4. Skeleton of a dolphin.

turn out sideways. When moving along normally the mole supports itself on the edge of the 'palm' and the side of the first toe.

Mammals have also become adapted for life in and under water. The simplest adaptation is the rows of stiff hairs which extend the surface of the hindfoot or form a keel-like ridge along the tail to aid swimming. Among insectivores this adaptation is found in water shrews (*Neomys*) for example, and in muskrats amongst the rodents. A more sophisticated adaptation is the webbing between the toes of the hindfeet of, for example, the Beaver and Coypu (rodents), and on both hind and forefeet of the Otter (a carnivore).

The greatest degree of adaptation to life in the water is seen in the marine mammals—seals, walruses, sea-lions, whales, dolphins etc. In the pinnipeds (seals, sea-lions, walruses) limbs have been transformed into structures resembling fins. Sea-lions and walruses can still 'walk' on these limbs which retain some supportive function on dry land. In seals (fig. 3) the hindlimbs have completely lost their supportive capacity, and are used simply for steering. The forelimbs are much reduced so that on dry land, seals can do no more than crawl and heave themselves about with great difficulty. The cetaceans (whales) are even more specialized, never leaving the water, and at first sight hardly resembling mammals at all. The forelimbs are shortened and modified to flippers which move only at the shoulder joint. The hind limbs have almost disappeared and only vestigial remnants of the pelvis can be seen in the skeleton (fig. 4).

Mammals have also mastered the air, whether in passive or active flight. Some members of the squirrel family are adapted for passive gliding flight. In the Russian Flying Squirrel a furred double membrane extends along the sides of the body; when the legs are extended it forms a 'parachute', allowing gliding flight of many tens of metres, during which the animal can even change direction. The only vertebrates capable of active flight (except birds) are the bats (order Chiroptera) (fig. 5). Their forelimbs

Fig. 5.   Bats (Chiroptera) are the only mammals capable of active flight.

are transformed into membranous wings which are supported by the bones of the arm and forearm and by the elongated 'fingers' with the exception of the thumb (fig. 1a). The wing surface consists of a thin double membrane, usually without fur, which connects the body to the limbs and, as a rule, the hindlimbs to the tail. At rest, bats either fold their wings along the body or wrap them around themselves. The hindlimbs are usually used only for hanging by. Only in some groups, the South American Vampire Bats, for example, are they also used for crawling. Naturally, special muscles used in flight have developed, and like birds, bats have a crest on the breastbone (sternum) to which the flight muscles are attached.

Feeding

Mammals eat many different kinds of food, and this is reflected in specialized adaptations of the digestive system. The mouth and teeth are the only parts that the amateur naturalist is likely to be able to examine. The tongue, a muscular organ, has become modified in various ways. In carnivores it bears hard horny papillae on the surface and is used like a rasp, for scraping off the remains of meat from bones. Carnivores also use the tongue for lapping up water. Many of the even-toed ungulates use the tongue for tearing off vegetation to eat. Many mammals groom themselves by licking with the tongue.

The number and shape of the teeth differ from species to species and are an important aid in identification. Young mammals develop an incomplete set of milk teeth which are replaced by a permanent set later on. Four types of teeth are distinguished. Taking the upper jaw first, the incisors (I) grow out of the intermaxillary bone, the canines (C) are the first teeth in the upper jaw proper, and the premolars (P) are next to the canines. All these teeth appear in the first set. Molars (M) are set behind the premolars and appear only in the permanent dentition. The teeth of the lower jaw are designated with reference to the corresponding tooth in the

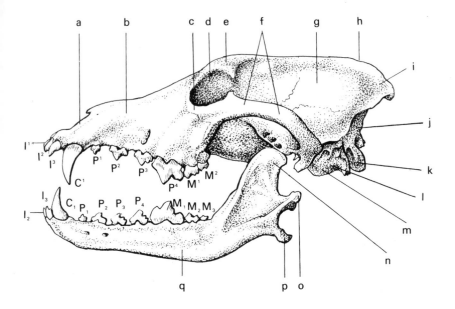

Fig. 6. Skull of a wolf: **a**, intermaxillary; **b**, upper jaw; **c**, cheekbone or zygomatic bone; **d**, eyehole (orbit); **e**, frontal bone; **f**, zygomatic arch; **g**, parietal bone; **h**, sagittal crest; **i**, interparietal bone; **j**, occipital bone; **k**, occipital condyle; **l**, external auditory passage; **m**, tympanic cavity; **n**, muscular process; **o**, condyloid process; **p**, angular process; **q**, mandible; **I**, incisors; **C**, canines; **P**, premolars; **M**, molars.

upper jaw and by similarities in shape to those of the upper jaw. A dental formula gives a concise indication of the number and type of teeth present. It is written as a fraction indicating the number of individual teeth of each type in one half of the upper and lower jaw. From left to right the order is incisors, canines, premolars, molars. The greatest number of teeth in placental mammals is 44, that is, 3 incisors, 1 canine, 4 premolars and 3 molars in each half of the jaw. The corresponding dental formula would be: $\dfrac{3143}{3143}$.

In various species, the number of teeth differs, usually corresponding to different modes of nutrition. In ruminants, for example, the upper incisors are missing. In the cats, as highly specialized flesh eaters, the number of molars and premolars is reduced — 3131. The lynx, for example, has only 2 premolars and 1 molar in each half jaw: 3121. In the beasts of prey generally, the last upper premolar and the first lower molar have become adapted for tearing, biting or crushing the prey; these are called the carnassial teeth. In rodents there is only one incisor in each half of the jaw; it is chisel-shaped and never stops growing.

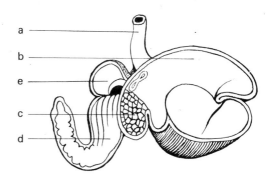

Fig. 7. Stomach of a ruminant in cross section: **a**, oesophagus; **b**, rumen; **c**, reticulum; **d**, omasum; **e**, abomasum.

The teeth of fish-eating mammals, such as seals, are remarkably uniform, and different tooth types can barely be distinguished. This trend is even more marked in the dolphins, which also have many more teeth than the typical mammals—up to 250 in some species. Whales and other cetaceans represent the opposite extreme, with some species lacking teeth altogether. In the baleen whales (suborder Mysticeti) embryonal teeth develop but never cut through the gums. Instead, horny plates develop from the roof of the mouth and hang down, acting as filters for the fine plankton on which these animals feed. These horny plates are the 'whalebone' or baleen. The whale feeds by taking a mouthful of water, the plankton caught by the baleen is conveyed by the tongue via the pharynx to the oesophagus, and the water escapes at the corners of the mouth. The Narwhal has only two teeth, a single canine in each half of the intermaxillary bone. In the male the left canine develops to form a single tusk up to 1 metre long. The Beluga, a member of the same order, has usually 8—10 teeth.

The mammalian stomach has also evolved differently in various species in response to various ways of feeding. The most complicated arrangement is found in ruminants, animals that chew the cud, in which there are four 'stomachs', through which the food passes in different stages of digestion (fig. 7). Food first enters the rumen, then the reticulum and the omasum and finally the true stomach, the abomasum. Divided stomachs are also found in other herbivores, in kangaroos, sloths and some leaf-eating monkeys. In all these animals the divided stomach is related to the fact that plant material needs lengthy digestion. It is interesting therefore that dolphins, flesh-eaters feeding mainly on fish, also have a divided stomach. In their case it relates to the fact that dolphins swallow their prey whole. In the first part of the stomach the food is mashed up by muscular contraction aided by sand and stones that the dolphin also swallows.

Although many mammals depend completely or partly on plant food, no mammal can produce the enzyme cellulase, which breaks down the cellulose in plant cell walls into digestible carbohydrates. In the herbivores, which depend entirely on plants for food, digestion of cellulose is vital, and it is broken down in their digestive tracts by the action of symbiotic bacteria and other microorganisms that do produce cellulase. In ruminants these bacteria are concentrated in the anterior stomach compartments, in other herbivores (horses, for example) the large intestine acts as a fermentation chamber, and the simple carbohydrate products of cellulose digestion are absorbed through the lining of its walls. Hares and some other rodents have other ways of getting the most out of their food. They excrete soft droppings composed of partially-digested food material which they then eat. The food is further digested and the characteristic hard droppings are excreted.

The shape of droppings is very characteristic for different species and is a useful aid to identification, allowing us not only to determine the species, but in some cases also the sex of the animal (in Red Deer).

Fur, horns and antlers

A furry or hairy coat is a mammalian characteristic found in no other group of animals. A mammal's coat is composed of two principal hair types, short fine dense hairs forming the undercoat and longer guard hairs. The undercoat insulates the animal and plays an important part in maintaining constant body temperature. The guard hairs determine the colour of the coat. In some mammals the fur is either very sparse or entirely lacking—the cetaceans are the most extreme example of this. Many mammals have long flexible tactile hairs, which are most familiar as the whiskers of rodents and carnivores. Squirrels bear similar tactile hairs on their flanks and forelimbs. The roots of these hairs are encased in blood vessels and when the animal is alerted the vessels become filled with blood and the hairs stand out from the body. Nerve endings close to the roots of tactile hairs sense their vibration. Other types of specialized hairs are numerous—eyelashes, bristles, and the hair of manes and tails are only a few examples.

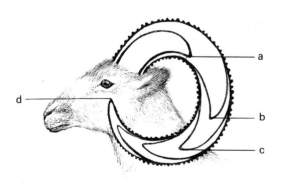

Fig. 8. Diagram of horn growth in the mouflon ram. The animal's age can be estimated by the curvature of the horn. On an imaginary clockface, the tip of the left sheath in a one-year-old ram points to about 1 o'clock (a), in a two-year-old ram to 3 o'clock (b), in a three-year-old (c) and older rams it always shows a time exceeding their actual age by 2 'hours'. This holds true until about the seventh year after which the tip invariably points to about 9 o'clock (d).

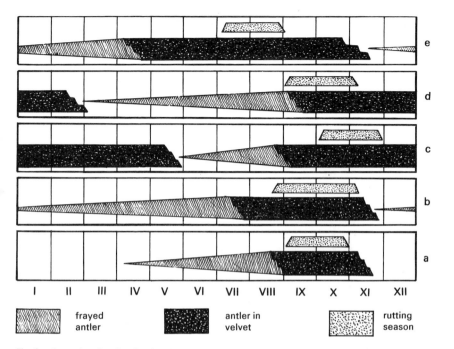

Fig. 9. Annual cycle of antler development in European
deer: a, Reindeer; b, Elk; c, Fallow Deer; d, Red Deer; e, Roe Deer

Key:
- frayed antler
- antler in velvet
- rutting season

Hair, horns and hooves, although very different in appearance, are composed of very similar materials. The spines of porcupines, the prickles of hedgehogs and the scales and armour plating of pangolins and armadillos are also variations on the same theme.

All horny structures arise originally from the skin (epidermis) and are composed of epidermal cells which have become *cornified*. The horns of bovids (oxen, gazelles, etc.) are permanent structures. Within the bovid family horns may develop in both sexes (Chamois, Bison, gazelles, Musk Ox), or in males only (Saiga, Mouflon). The basis of the horn is an outgrowth of the frontal bone of the skull which is encased in a sheath of cornified epidermis. Cornification of the epidermis at the base of the horn proceeds continually, pushing the older parts outwards. Each annual accretion of horn is marked by a thickened ring on the surface and so the animal's age can often be reliably determined by counting the number of rings on the horn (fig. 8).

Except for the most primitive genera, most members of the deer family bear antlers. These develop in males only, except in Reindeer, in which both males and females have antlers, pregnant females shedding their antlers only after giving birth to the young rather than at the normal time.

Antlers are bony, developing from projections on the frontal bone called pedicels or 'knobs'. The growing antler is covered with 'velvet', a layer of skin and tissue (corium), rich in blood vessels, which supplies the antler with nourishment. When growth is complete this layer dries up and the animal removes it by rubbing against branches. At a certain time the layer of bone between the pedicel and the antler proper breaks down and the antlers are shed. The growth and shedding of antlers is in general influenced by hormones—the antler is fully developed and the velvet removed by the beginning of the rutting season. There are some exceptions, especially in tropical deer species which keep their antlers for several seasons. In contrast, some deer species grow two sets of antlers each year (Père David's Deer, *Elaphurus davidianus*, and *Cervus elaphus xanthopygus*). Antler development in European deer is shown in fig. 9. The timing is somewhat different in old and young stags — older ones shed their antlers earlier than younger ones.

Behaviour

Present-day thinking considers animal behaviour to be determined by a potential range of genetically-determined instinctive responses which can be elicited by stimuli coming from the external environment and from the animal's own internal physiology, and which can also be modified to a greater or lesser extent by learning based on experience. In many mammals particularly, learning is of considerable importance. Behaviour is often categorized into various functional types such as: (1) that concerned with movement; (2) that concerned with basic bodily functions — feeding, excretion, rest and sleep; (3) care of the coat — grooming; (4) defence and protection; (5) orientation in space — how does the animal find its way around; (6) orientation in time; (7) territorial behaviour; (8) building activity — constructing nests or lairs; (9) exploring the environment; (10) learning on the basis of experience; (11) play; (12) behaviour surrounding reproduction; (13) communication. These categories are mainly for convenience. In reality a particular piece of behaviour can be studied from many different points of view.

The analysis of the natural behaviour of a wild animal in terms of the environmental stimuli that evoke it is a difficult task requiring long and detailed observation of the animal in the field. Instinctive behaviour is elicited in certain conditions by stimuli which are often designated release or evoking mechanisms. The complex behaviour of mammals is the result of many interrelated and complementary release mechanisms, and the external stimuli are often extremely subtle and difficult for the human observer to recognize. For certain kinds of behaviour to occur not only must the external stimuli be present but the animal must be physiologically 'prepared' or attuned to receive and act upon them.

This is most obvious in reproductive behaviour. A well-studied example is that of the mating behaviour of Red Deer stags. The genetically-determined action of sexual hormones prepares the animals for reproduction at a certain time of the year. Towards the end of August, Red Deer stags start 'fraying' their antlers (clearing them of velvet) and change their way of life. So far they have lived solitarily or in groups of stags, now they seek the company of the hinds. They round up the hinds and stake claim to a territory by roaring, to announce to other males that they intend to defend it. Like most ruminants, Red Deer are essentially lone animals that keep a certain distance from each other and normally avoid close physical contact. The mating ceremonial has presumably developed for breaking through this instinctive distancing behaviour to make reproduction possible. At first Red Deer females run from the male and refuse his advances. But their hormones too are preparing them for reproduction. The Red Deer stag continually checks his hinds' preparedness and therefore their eventual willingness to mate by sniffing their urine (in which sex hormones are excreted) and can recognize the point at which the level of sex hormones is high enough. This is a striking piece of behaviour, known as *flehmen*. The male sniffs or licks at the female's urine, lifts his head, slightly opens his mouth and rolls up his upper lip. Scent stimuli are detected by a special organ on the upper palate (Jacobson's organ, present in many vertebrates). When the signs are right, the male attempts a further approach to the female. He makes a wooing gesture, a soft, slow stroking between the female's hindlegs with his stretched foreleg. If the female is ready to mate, this makes her adopt the mating posture, standing rigidly with her neck slightly stretched forward, back arched and hindlegs apart. The female's mating posture elicits the actual mating behaviour by the male, who stands up on his hindlegs, embraces the female's loins with his forelegs and mates with her.

In this case the interaction between physiological receptiveness and instinctive responses to certain well-defined series of stimuli produce a clear-cut behaviour. The example shows how an animal in a state of physiological attunement will begin to search for the release mechanisms calling forth the appropriate instinctive behaviour. However, an external stimulus will not evoke a particular behaviour if the animal is not attuned to it. The above example also shows how behaviour influences the behavioural signals coming from another animal, or from the inanimate environment, thus setting up a complete behaviour pattern.

Communication

Mammals are highly effective communicators, having many different ways of expressing their 'feelings' and intentions by posture, body movement, facial expressions, sound and scent. Many of these responses, such as bristling up the fur when danger threatens, are innate automatic responses to a stimulus, similar to those that govern simple instinctive actions. Gregarious mammals have much more sophisticated communication systems than those living solitarily. The gregarious Wolf, for example, has around 40 per cent more different communication signals than the solitary Fox.

Mammals communicate by visual signals, sound and smell. They have a wide range of visual signals, whereas communication by sound is less well-developed generally than it is, say, in birds. Communication by scent cues is more difficult for the human observer to recognize but is probably very widespread and typical. Communication signals are primarily intended for members of the same species although they may be recognized by members of other species. This applies particularly to alarm signals. The warning whistle of the Marmot elicits a reaction from the Chamois, a rabbit's warning thump is widely understandable, to the Roe Deer for instance, that also takes to flight. Virtually all mammals have innate mechanisms that prevent members of the same species from killing each other. Only man—who has awarded himself the epithet *sapiens* (rational)—has apparently lost these inhibitions and resorts to war and murder.

Visual signals include posture, mimicry, facial expression, change in the body's outline and colour. The animal may also leave behind visual signs effective even in its absence—heaps of faeces or droppings in a conspicuous place (horse and weasel families), gnawed-off branches (squirrels), or a rubbed tree (bear, bison). A raised head, lifted tail and a stiff, accentuated gait are alarm signals in a great many species of ungulates. Bristling fur on the back or rump, often accentuated by conspicuous colouring, is a warning signal easily understandable even to us. Neither do we require any detailed explanation when beasts of prey, and primates also, bare their teeth. To see how such behaviour develops, let us take as an example some members of the cervine family. The upper jaw of primitive deer species (e.g. the Chinese Water Deer or the Muntjac) is equipped with strongly developed, long sharp canines which serve as effective weapons. To produce a threatening expression they turn up their lip and show these canines to the enemy. In the course of evolutionary development, canines in other deer species have lost their function and have either become stunted or disappeared completely. In Red Deer the canines (tusks) are quite small, in Fallow Deer or Roe Deer they have disappeared. However the original behaviour has been preserved and, when expressing threat, these species turn up their upper lip to exhibit their non-existent weapons. And nature has gone yet further: in a number of species which lack canines, a conspicuous light-coloured spot has developed on the lower lip which mimics the missing canines.

Communication by sound can occur over much greater distances, and even when the animals cannot see each other. A large repertoire of sound signals is found, for example, in the dog family (especially in its gregarious species), in apes, and in dolphins among the cetaceans. The range of sounds produced by mammals is enormous. Some are barely discernible, such as the chirping of some insectivores and bats; others, on the contrary, are loud and powerful, such as the roaring of Red Deer stags in rut, the howling of Wolves, or the whistling of the Marmot. The extraordinary and beautiful siren-like sounds produced by the Humpback Whale are audible over distances of up to 100 km.

Some mammals make sounds the human ear cannot hear. We can perceive tones with a frequency of approximately 20 kHz, allowing for individual variability as well as the fact that, with advancing age, we cannot hear sounds near the upper limit of perception. One group of mammals that uses ultrasound are the bats (chiropterans). Through their partially opened mouth some bats send out a series of very short sounds at a frequency of 30—70 kHz, each lasting no more than two or three thousandths of a second. These sound waves are reflected from any nearby object and intercepted by the bat's auditory organ. With this means of echolocation, bats can precisely localize an object in space. Horseshoe bats possess an even more perfect system of sound orientation: in contrast to 'evening' bats (Vespertilionidae), they transmit ultrasound through their nose, regulating it by special membranous growths. The frequency of these signals is 80—100 kHz (that is, 80,000—100,000 oscillations per second!), and their reflection returns to the animal before the signal itself has ceased. Even man with all his technical know-how has not been able to better this. If in the early evening you come across a flying bat, listen carefully: you will probably hear a thin 'squeak' at the verge of audibility if the bat is 'transmitting' at the lower limit of its frequency range. Southern Europe is the home of a great many bat species, and they have attracted particular attention in places where they appear in large numbers. One appealing observation by an ancient Greek writer has come down to us: 'Bats address themselves to young people. When a person grows old, they do not fall silent—it is only his ear that hardens.' Bats were the first mammals in which orientation by ultrasound was established. A similar mode of orientation was later found in some insectivores and rodents. Echolocation has been thoroughly studied in cetaceans, especially in dolphins. Where echolocation occurs in an aquatic environment, we speak of hydrolocation. Dolphins are well-adapted for marine life and their 'ears' are hidden, but despite this their hearing is perfect. The bones, cavities and oil-filled hollows of the skull, and even the jaws, are all involved in the transmission of sound waves. The frequency of sounds emitted and received by dolphins ranges from 4 to 300 kHz. This upper limit is exceptional and the normal upper limit is lower, at approximately 120—180 kHz. The hydrolocation field varies according to individual species (fig. 10). Not all cetaceans are endowed with such fine vocal powers: some tend to produce sounds only rarely. Considering only sounds lying within the range of human hearing, one of the most 'loquacious' species is the Beluga, which the old whalers used to call the 'sea canary'.

Olfactory signals have a very wide application. They are used to mark

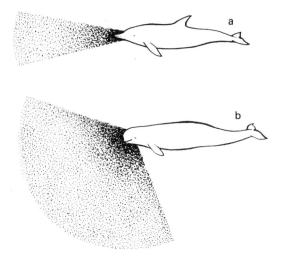

Fig. 10. Extent of the hydrolocation field in the dolphin (a) and in the beluga (b).

the individual's home range and its runways, they regulate sexual behaviour, express the animal's individual and social position, and serve as means of communication between individuals—particularly between mother and young. Olfactory signals can be secondarily applied as defence mechanisms, as in skunks (*Mephitis*) or the Polecat (*Putorius*).

Mammals often use their urine for marking a territory. Everyone is familiar with the dog marking conspicuous or important objects along the boundary of its territory, such as corner-stones, trees and lamp-posts. They are parsimonious with their urine to make it suffice for as many marks as possible. Not even the thousands of years of coexistence with man and all the transformations leading to such different breeds as the mastiff and the Pekinese, have succeeded in changing the dog's inborn behaviour which does not differ in the least from that of its wild ancestor the Wolf. Through artificial selection man has only succeeded in putting some dogs at a disadvantage. The manner of marking coincidentally provides evidence of the dog's rank. The higher the mark, that means, the higher the dog's urine can reach, the more effective is it and dogs incapable of urinating as high must withdraw from the territory as the weaker members in this contest. The dog family is not the only one to use urine to mark its territories. Horses do so, as do rhinoceros, many primates and some squirrel species amongst others. Sometimes the objects are not marked directly with the urine, but it is transferred onto them. Bisons, for example, first strip the bark off a tree with their horns, then urinate on the ground, wallow the tuft of hair covering their head in the urine, and finally rub off the mud together with the urine on the debarked tree. Some monkeys, such as the South American squirrel monkeys, urinate on their paws and subsequently leave a strongly smelling mark at every step. Examples are also known of males marking members of their herd, especially adult females, with urine. Males of some deer and antelope species urinate between their extended legs onto the lower edge of the mane on their throats which they subsequently rub against the females' back. Many rodents mark their females by urine directly: the male stands up on his hindlegs and sprinkles his female with a thin, well-aimed streamlet of urine. This kind of behaviour may also be observed in the guinea-pig and in rabbits (who are non-rodents).

Mammals also use their faeces as markings. The most usual way is to deposit droppings in particular, usually easily noticeable places. Mustelids (weasels and stoats) deposit their droppings on stones and stumps. Horses drop heaps of dung on the circumference of their territory.

Very many mammals use secretions from specialized scent glands for marking. In most carnivores, scent glands are situated on both sides of the anal opening and their secretions are discharged as the animal defecates, giving the faeces a characteristic odour. In some cases, as in the Marten, the animal also rubs its hind parts against conspicuous objects along the boundaries of its territory, often balancing upside-down on its forelegs in order to place its mark as high as possible. In polecats, and notoriously in skunks, these glands are very large indeed and are furnished with a special muscle enabling the animal, when in danger, to eject the secretion a relatively long way. A similar mechanism also occurs in the civet family, for example in the Feline or Small-spotted Genet.

In mammals scent glands may also be located on the head, on the flanks, on the tail and on the limbs (fig. 11). Deer have glands in front of the eyes (preocular glands), which in the rutting season swell up considerably and exude a tarry secretion which the animals deposit on tree trunks and branches. These glands also have an important function in Red Deer calves. The calves do not follow their mother immediately after birth but remain concealed in the undergrowth where, for the first three weeks, their mother returns only for the short periods needed to suckle them. In

Fig. 11. Scent glands in Roe Deer: **a**, between antlers; **b**, under tail; **c**, heel; **d**, in the cleft of the hoof.

23

order to reduce to the minimum the danger of disclosing the calf's hiding place, the calf drinks rapidly and the mother takes herself off as soon as she stops feeding. When the calf starts sucking, its preocular glands are wide open and the scent freely oozes out. As the stomach gradually fills up the glands gradually close and the olfactory signal begins to diminish and finally ceases completely. This tells the mother that the calf has had enough milk, and thus keeps the time during which the young is exposed to danger to a minimum.

The roebuck has a large scent gland between his antlers (fig. 11); in the Chamois it is located on the top of the head, behind the horns. Both species rub their heads against the branches of shrubs and trees, leaving an olfactory signal for other members of the species. Muntjacs have similar glands on their forehead. Some members of the squirrel family (e. g. the Souslik, the Marmot and the Eutamias) have scent glands in the cheeks. These are also rubbed against various objects to deposit scent signs marking out the boundary of the individual's home range. Hares also have scent glands in their cheeks but use them in quite a different way. The glands are on the inner surface of the cheeks, inside the mouth. When cleaning itself the hare covers its front paws with saliva mixed with the cheek-gland secretion and spreads it over its head; the scent remaining on the paws also marks each step of the hare's pathways and runs. In rabbits the scent gland is located on the lower jaw. The rabbit uses its secretion to mark twigs it has been gnawing.

Especially in ungulates, there may be scent glands of several types on the limbs. In members of the deer family, a gland bearing a brush of hairs is located on the inner side of the hind tibia. With each step this gland is wiped against grass and low undergrowth, leaving behind an olfactory signal. Glands may occur between the cleaves of both fore- and hindfeet (e.g. in Red Deer, Chamois and Mouflon), or of hindfeet only (e.g. in Roe Deer). Wild Goats and Barbary Sheep have developed such glands only between the cleaves of their forefeet. Sheep, Mouflons and gazelles have large inguinal (groin) glands whose function has so far not been fully explained.

Glands located on the flanks of some insectivores (e.g. shrews) and rodents (e.g. the Water Vole) attract considerable attention. In the breeding period they extend into a loaf-like swelling and intensify their secretion. These glands also serve for marking territory. Tail glands are found for example in members of the dog family. On the first third of the tail, on the upper surface, there is a gland known (e.g. in foxes) as 'violet'. Its location is indicated by a cluster of darker-coloured hairs. Some ungulates (e.g. Red Deer) also have scent glands on their tails.

Mammalian communities

What sort of communities do mammals form? Quite a number of species lead a solitary life and it is only in the breeding season that many individuals gather together. Hamsters (*Cricetus*), bears (*Ursus*) and wolverines (*Gulo*) are examples of such a hermit-like existence. However, the majority of mammals form communities of some kind, associating in various ways with individuals of the same species. A relatively rare type of association is an open anonymous group of individuals; any individual is free to leave the group at any time and another may join it. This type of community occurs, for example in the Mountain Hare (*Lepus timidus*). A second type is a closed anonymous group. This usually arises from a smaller group which, through continued reproduction, becomes so numerous that individual members do not know each other directly but recognize their affiliation to the group by a distinctive odour. Such 'families' of mice and Brown Rats (*Rattus norvegicus*) are well-known. If an individual is temporarily isolated from such a group, it is mercilessly attacked or killed after coming back. If, on the other hand, a complete stranger previously scented with the group odour is introduced into the group, it is accepted straight away. The most sophisticated type of community is one in which all individuals know each other — the family, the herd, or the school. Such a community can be formed by groups of individuals of both sexes, or by groups of males on the one hand, and groups of females with young on the other. Such separate communities can be permanent (in elephants, females and their young live permanently separated from the males), or seasonal, outside the rutting season only, as in Red Deer. While there are frequent conflicts among members of 'anonymous' communities, animals living in more closely-bonded communities suppress manifestations of aggression by a hierarchical ranking which determines the relative 'social' position of each member in the community. Members assume either a dominant or a submissive position. At the top of the social hierarchy we find the leader of the group, the strongest and most experienced animal. In some species this is a male, in others a female. From the leader of the community (designated as alpha), animals are ranked down to the individual with the lowest social status — omega. Position in the social scale is not necessarily constant, and can change, for example, throughout the year, according to the development of the young, and also perhaps to the physiological condition of adult members. For example, in Red Deer it is the rule that the social position of females in rut and of pregnant females automatically rises. Also, after the strongest stag in the group has shed his antlers, he loses his privileged position and is exposed to challenge from far weaker but still antlered stags. Ways of expressing social position vary from species to species. However, they always involve certain basic types of behaviour: threatening or imposing behaviour, postures and gestures of submission, and reconciliatory movements or pacifying behaviour.

Mammalian tracks and traces

Animal tracks are only left in certain conditions — soft, muddy ground or snow for example — and so may never be apparent in particular types of terrain or at certain times of year. It is far more likely that one will find traces of mammals by their droppings. It is relatively easy to distinguish carnivore droppings from those of herbivores, but it is not always so simple to identify the species concerned. For those mammals which have been hunted by man for thousands of years, much lore on their tracks and identification of their droppings exists. But relatively little is known about the tracks and droppings of small mammals: with a few exceptions, we can only establish the broad category of animal — whether it is a mouse or a vole, a large weasel or a small stoat, and so on. Far more telling is the environment in which the respective traces and signs are found. The most helpful clues are traces of other activities such as feeding damage and the remains of meals.

Feeding damage is most frequently found on trunks and branches of trees or shrubs. Its location and size often help us to identify its originator. Near the ground, up to a height of 70 cm at most, tooth marks of hares or rabbits may be found — especially where the ground is covered with deep snow in winter. In subtropical regions, browsing damage caused by hares is a rare sight. Feeding damage found higher up the trunk indicates ungulates. Traces of Mouflons' browsing are easily recognizable: grooves slanting in both directions. Red Deer either peel off the bark in strips, loosening a part of the bark with their lower incisors and jerking their head to tear off a strip upwards, or leave behind relatively small irregular grooves on one side of the trunk only. Smaller trees with bark peeled off all round probably indicate Roe Deer. Bison also like tree bark: they peel off strips reaching several metres above the ground.

Traces of feeding damage may be found even in the branches of trees. Longitudinal scratch marks only on the bark betray the activity of Bank Voles or field mice. If, as well as the bark, the underlying layer of wood has also been gnawed, the squirrel has been at work here. Smaller scratch marks across the branches are characteristic of dormice. Squirrels and dormice are both particularly fond of nibbling away buds.

In spruce forests we often come across gnawed-off cones — these are traces of either squirrels or field mice feeding. It is fairly easy to distinguish between the two. Field mice and Bank Voles bite off the seed scales of conifers cleanly at their base, close to the cone stem. Squirrels, on the other hand, leave longer, irregular scale remnants.

Underneath stones, in cavities in trees, and in other hiding places we frequently find acorns, pips or seeds, sometimes in large quantities. The particular way in which they have been opened enables us to determine what animal gathered and hid them. Hazelnuts are particularly good for identifying the animal involved. A squirrel first gnaws a small opening, wedges its lower incisors into the nut and cracks it open. A field mouse gnaws a large opening on one end of the nut; the outer edge bears many marks made by the upper incisors. Bank Voles make a similar hole but with a smoother edge and no incisor marks on the outside of the shell. Voles and Water Voles, whoenever they can reach the nuts, gnaw a hole in the side of the shell.

Carnivorous animals also occasionally leave behind signs of feeding, especially on the eggs of ground-nesting birds. These remains can easily be distinguished from the eggs broken, for example, by crows which also occasionally ravage birds' nests. Whereas crows leave the broken eggshells in large pieces, in a nest demolished by a hedgehog we find only small bits of shattered eggshell, and the whole nest soiled by the contents of the eggs. Sometimes eggs are found with holes at both ends. This is the way in which weasels and stoats get to the food inside. Larger mustelids (e.g. martens and polecats) usually take the egg away from the nest to eat it in some secluded spot. They leave the eggshell with a large, angular opening in its side.

Interesting traces of feeding activity may be found along the banks of lakes and streams. This particularly applies where abundant plant remains have been left behind by some rodents. Beside the remains of chewed or gnawed-off stalks and leaves, droppings may also be found; from their size, we can quite easily determine whether the animal feasting here was a Water Vole or a Muskrat. The Muskrat also has a habit of discarding bivalve shells, bearing the marks of its teeth, in one place. It gathers mussels from the bottom, pries them open with its teeth and eats their fleshy leg. Remains of fish may sometimes be found at the waterside. If the head is missing, or if nothing but the tail and larger bones have been left behind, we may be fairly sure that the Otter was making a meal here. If only the underpart of the fish is missing, it was probably eaten by a polecat.

Sometimes we do not find food remains themselves but traces made by the animal in its search for food. The Wild Boar leaves traces of digging in meadows and fields. When it has been rooting for a vole it leaves a row of dug-up turfs. When rummaging for potatoes in a field, it leaves behind long furrows. Small mounds of earth on the surface of a meadow — molehills — betray the activity of moles. Smaller and less regular 'molehills' are the work of water voles. At first sight, molehills might easily be confused with the mounds of earth heaped on the surface by mole rats. However, closer examination will reveal that these are piled up beside a burrow.

In steppes, semi-deserts or deserts one may find small conical hollows dug at an angle in the ground. These are evidence of the nocturnal visits of jerboas (*Allactaga, Jaculus*) searching for food. In sandy terrain, in the early morning one can find misshapen 'mudpies' covering up the entrances into the burrows of these interesting rodents.

Small tunnels and runways are sometimes discernible in low vegetation, in grass or in moss. These are paths used by voles and bank voles for running to and fro between their burrows. Such passages in the moss of the tundra are sure to be pathways of the Norwegian Lemming. Other lemming species burrow their tunnels just beneath the surface of the ground.

Mammals also leave traces when engaged in other activities, such as marking. Marks formed by droppings have already been discussed. Stripped-off bark does not always indicate feeding damage. Roe Deer (with a large scent gland between their antlers) and Chamois (with one on the nape of the neck, behind the horns), both damage trees as they rub the glands against branches and trunks of small shrubs. The roebuck most frequently makes this kind of damage at the time he is cleaning his antlers. He often leaves behind a thin clean-stripped trunk with, at its base, litter scraped from the ground, his antler cleaning is accompanied by energetic pawing of the ground with his foreleg.

Remnants of the removed 'velvet' can be found directly on the trunk or below it. Red Deer fraying their antlers cause similar, though more extensive, damage to shrubs, which are often broken down to the ground. In areas where bears still exist we may come across bark strips which include the layers of bast or phloem. Here we may often find imprints of the bear's claws on the bark, and also traces of its fur. The bear, having removed the bark, turns its back to the trunk to rub its fur against the damaged place.

Saigas and gazelles bite off tips of twigs or of strong grass stems and, having modified them in this way, mark them with scent from their preocular glands. Because they are ruminants, with no incisors in their upper jaw, the branch tips are raggedly bitten off. Red Deer mark with the exudate from their preocular glands but they only rub it onto trunk or branches without marking the severed ends of twigs. There is in fact no possibility of confusion as the animals do not inhabit the same environment.

Finally — if one discovers a tree cavity whose mouth is surrounded by flies, it is almost sure to be the hideaway of some bat species.

Only a few of the characteristic mammalian marks and signs have been mentioned here. The art of reading animal tracks and markings in the wild requires many years' experience and a talent for observation. It is, however, an important skill to acquire in order to get to know mammalian wildlife. So cultivate patience, which, in this field, is indispensable.

How to observe and study mammals

It is much more difficult to observe mammals than, say, birds. For the most part, mammals mainly come out at dusk or at night, and this in itself makes observation very difficult. Moreover, the populations of many mammalian species are rather sparse, and so individuals may only rarely be encountered. The least difficult to observe are ungulates, especially those living in open country. Field glasses are essential. In most cases, ungulates living in forests or woodland come out at a certain time of day to the wood edges, clearings or fields in search for food, and can then be seen. One must become familiar with the animal's routine which, however, is subject to change with the season of the year and with age and condition of the animal. Animals are often much easier to observe during the mating season (rut), when they are more active and may more easily be approached. In the mating season a great many species attract attention by the sounds they make.

It is much more difficult to observe carnivores. With a few exceptions their population density is small and they live in strict seclusion. As a rule, nothing but traces of their activity can be found in the wild — footprints in snow, mud, soft soil or sand, or most commonly, their droppings, often deposited in conspicuous places as a visual and olfactory mark. In such a place one can then lie in wait for the animal. It is also possible to prepare a bait at an appropriate spot. One can also wait near burrows and hiding places, or near the most clearly marked pathways.

As far as the smaller, solitary mammals are concerned, it is usual to find only footprints or droppings, feeding damage and remains of meals. In such cases we can only wait patiently in a suitable spot. With luck one may have the opportunity eventually to see, for example, the Muskrat, the Bank Vole, or the Water Shrew.

Animals living in colonies are somewhat easier to spot. With a few exceptions, such species are active at certain times of day. The greater number of individuals inhabiting a given area increases the possibility of seeing an animal. This is the case, for example, for Marmots or Sousliks. Small rodent species living in colonies also have smaller flight distances, that is the distance which they have to overcome when escaping from danger. On the whole it is fairly easy to observe life in a colony of voles or lemmings. Squirrels may also be observed without great difficulties, particularly where they have become accustomed to humans, for example in parks, gardens and cemeteries. With sufficient patience, one can even observe the activity of the mole whose active periods alternate with approximately three half-hour periods of rest.

Among nocturnal mammals, hedgehogs are the easiest to observe. They make a lot of noise when moving about so that it does not require much skill to find them, and they do not run away. In late summer, the Edible or Fat Dormouse may be observed by night in orchards with ripening fruit. In places where it occurs it is usually relatively abundant. As it frequently makes itself heard in the branches, it is not difficult to catch sight of it in the beam of a strong torch.

Breeding colonies of seals and bats' breeding and hibernation colonies are only mentioned here for completeness. These animals are already in serious danger from human interference and we ask you not to disturb them further by any attempt at close observation, however careful you may be.

There are a great many small mammals that we may encounter in the wild by chance, and yet wish to study. There is no other way than to try to catch these animals alive by some humane method and keep them at home in captivity. Traps for catching small living mammals are usually not available to buy and it is easiest to make one oneself. One type is a box with a trapdoor which is released when the animal enters. Far simpler and very effective is a pit-trap, for example a broad-mouthed large jar or bottle sunk in the ground close to the surface. It is best to cover such a trap with a piece of bark, wood, or a flat stone, otherwise the trapped animal may be drowned in water accumulated during rainfall. Box traps are usually baited with root vegetables, oil-rich seeds, bread etc., depending on the species we are trying to catch. Pitfalls may but need not be baited: animals usually fall into them accidentally.

It is important to remember that many species are protected by law in most European countries. Protected species are chiefly insectivores and a few rodents. Bats are protected almost everywhere. It is forbidden to disturb them and no-one should catch them without a special licence. Various protective or hunting laws have also been issued to protect many large mammals. It is therefore advisable to become acquainted in advance with the regulations in one's own country and any other country one intends to visit.

Taking photographs of mammals in their natural environment is an extremely demanding hobby requiring special telephoto lenses, electronic flash, a great deal of patience, and large quantities of film. Very few pictures turn out well enough to be useful as documentation. Good, close-up photographs of mammals in the wild are rare.

No amateur naturalist, we hope, would deliberately kill an animal in order to study it, except perhaps for the few pest species such as mice, Brown Rats, Common Voles, and a few other rodents. Occasionally, however, one may find a dead body of a rare or interesting species and wish to preserve it for further study by experts. The best method is to store it in a 4—6 per cent formalin solution, or in a 70—80 per cent alcohol solution. If neither formalin nor alcohol are available, a short-term emergency measure is to preserve the body in a saturated solution of kitchen salt. It is particularly important to give as much information as possible about the material. A label recording the date and place of the find as well as the name of the collector is best attached to the hindpaw. One should include a good description of the locality in which it was found, the height above sea level, type of terrain etc. and also the circumstances of the find. A soft pencil should be used for writing the description so that it will not become illegible in the fixing solution. Before putting the animal in the fixative it is advisable to make a small incision into the ventral cavity enabling the solution to penetrate deep into the body, and so prevent its eventual decomposition. We can then hand our find over to a museum for further study.

How to measure mammals

All measurements should be taken according to well-defined and gener-
ally-agreed on standards so that results from different animals are
directly comparable.

For measuring smaller mammals it is best to use calipers or dividers.
Calipers 20—25 cm long are the most useful and convenient for field-work.
A measuring tape is used for larger animals. Small mammals are best
measured with their underside uppermost. Adjust the body to an approximately natural position, without stretching it too much. The length of head
and body (Lhb) is measured from the tip of the nose to the anal opening.
The length of the tail (Lt) is measured from the anal opening to the tip of
the tail, without taking into account any long terminal hairs. The length of
the hindpaw (Lhp) is measured along the leg bent at the heel joint, and is
the distance between the back edge of the heel joint and the tip of the
longest toe not counting the claw. The length of the auricle (external ear)
(Le) is measured on the inside and is the distance between the lower
notch of the auricle to the tip. Ignore any tufts of hairs at the tip of the ear.
Some mammals, shrews for example, have tiny ears and in such cases, as
a rule, this dimension is not recorded. For identifying bats and horseshoe
bats it is essential to know the length of the forearm (Lf). This is measured
from the wrist joint to the back edge of the elbow joint. For an exact identification of some bat species we must also know the length of the membranous lid in their ear (tragus) (Ltr). This is measured from its lower to
its upper end.

For larger mammals the length of head and body (Lhb) is measured
along the back from the tip of the nose to the base of the tail (not to the
anal opening, as is the case in small mammals) with the measuring tape fol-

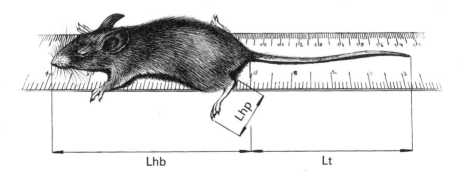

Fig. 12. Measuring small mammals: **Lhb**, head and body length;
Lt, tail length; **Lhp**, length of the sole of the hindfoot.

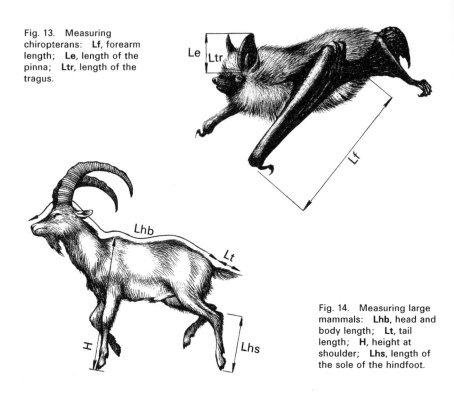

Fig. 13. Measuring chiropterans: **Lf**, forearm length; **Le**, length of the pinna; **Ltr**, length of the tragus.

Fig. 14. Measuring large mammals: **Lhb**, head and body length; **Lt**, tail length; **H**, height at shoulder; **Lhs**, length of the sole of the hindfoot.

lowing the curves of the body. The length of the tail (Lt) is then measured from the base of the tail to its tip, excluding terminal hairs. The length of the hind sole (Lhs) in ungulates is measured from the heel joint to the hoof tips. Ear length (Le) is measured as before. In ungulates, another measure is taken: the height at the shoulder (H). This is the distance between the tip of the foreleg and the highest place on the back in the region of the shoulder-blade. For a systematic evaluation of cetaceans a number of dimensions are recorded which take into account the anatomical peculiarities of these aquatic mammals. For our purposes it will be sufficient to know the total length (L) measured from the tip of the snout to the end of the body (i.e. without the overlapping lateral lobes of the anal fin).

The weight (W) is usually obtained by direct weighing. A letter scale is commonly used for weighing small mammals and a spring balance for larger ones.

Key for the identification of orders and families of European mammals

1 hoofed **2**

without hoofs **6**

2 a single hoof on each foot. . . . .
    Order: Perissodactyla
    Family: **Equidae**

even number of hoofs on each foot **3**
    Order: Artiodactyla

3 soles with large ligamental pads,
small hoofs on toe tips . . . .
    Family: **Camelidae**

small hoofs fully covering toes, sole surface hard **4**

4 long muzzle terminating in a flat, cartilaginous plate, canines
in both jaws elongated . . . .
    Family: **Suidae**

muzzle differently formed, incisors absent from upper jaw **5**

5 besides hoofs, dew claws on the back
of the leg . . . .
    Family: **Cervidae**

two hoofs only on each foot,
dew claws absent . . . .
    Family: **Bovidae**

6 toes provided with nails . . . .
    Order: Primates
    Family: **Cercopithecidae**

toes provided with claws. **7**

7 forefoot not resembling a paw, toes very long,
connected by a flying membrane **8**
    Order: Chiroptera

toes on forefoot relatively short,
foot resembles a paw or a fin. **10**

8 membranous outgrowths on nose............................
    Family: **Rhinolophidae**

no membranous outgrowths on nose,
variously shaped membranous outgrowth
(lid, tragus) in the ear.. **9**

9 tail not longer than the flying membrane,
or only the tip projecting...................................
    Family: **Vespertilionidae**

tail very long, extending
far beyond the flying membrane ....
    Family: **Molossidae**

10 forefoot resembling a paw **11**

forefoot resembling a fin... **33**

11 animal resembles a rabbit or a hare ....
    Order: Lagomorpha
    Family: **Leporidae**

bears no resemblance to a rabbit or a hare **12**

12 pair of chisel-shaped incisors in upper
jaw, a gap between incisors and other teeth **13**
    Order: Rodentia

chisel-shaped incisors absent from
upper jaw, no gap between incisors
and other teeth **23**

13 toes of hindpaws webbed **14**

toes of hindpaws not webbed **15**

14 tail broad and flat,
covered with scaly skin ....
    Family: **Castoridae**

tail circular in cross-section ....
    Family: **Myocastoridae**

15 tailless, cylindrical body, auricles absent,
eyes covered with skin...................................
    Family: **Spalacidae**

tail of various lengths **16**

16 back and tail covered with long spines . . . .
    Family: **Hystricidae**

    back and tail without spines, exceptionally fur on the back interspersed with
    spiny hairs, the animal resembling a mouse **17**

17 hind legs very long, about
    four times as long as forelegs.
    Long tail terminating in a flag . . . .
    Family: **Dipodidae**

    hindlegs shorter, at most twice as long as forelegs. Tail always without flag . . **18**

18 upper lip not split . . . .
    Family: **Zapodidae**

    upper lip split **19**

19 tail covered with thick fur or long bristles **20**

    tail covered with short and sparse fur or almost bare **22**

20 tail short, with long bristles. Stiff hairs
    on hindpaw, arranged comb-like, covering claws . . . .
    Family: **Ctenodactylidae**

    tail either long or short but always covered with dense,
    often shaggy fur. Hindpaw without comb-like hairs **21**

21 3 molars in each half of the jaw. Diurnal
    (except for the Flying Squirrel) . . . .
    Family: **Sciuridae**

    4 molars in each half of the jaw. Nocturnal . . . .
    Family: **Gliridae**

22 molars with 2 longitudinal rows of cusps or
    transverse ridges, or with flat crowns running
    out into triangular projections on the sides . . . .
    Family: **Cricetidae**

    molars with 3 rows of cusps, the middle row
    being the highest . . . .
    Family: **Muridae**

23 large, strongly projecting canines, small number of molars **24**
Order: Carnivora

small canines, numerous molars **30**
Order: Insectivora

24 hindfoot with 5 toes **25**

hindfoot with 4 toes **28**

25 large-sized mammals, body length exceeding 150 cm,
tail very short, seems to be missing altogether . . . .
Family: **Ursidae**

small- to medium-sized mammals, body length
up to 100 cm but usually much smaller, tail distinct,
at least 1/10 of body length, but usually longer **26**

26 2 molars in upper jaw behind the carnassial
(last premolar, second longest tooth after the canine) **27**

1 molar in upper jaw behind
the carnassial . . . .
Family: **Mustelidae**

27 short legs; long slender body . . . .
Family: **Viverridae**

moderately long legs; thickset body . . . .
Family: **Procyonidae**

28 sharp, retractile claws . . . .
Family: **Felidae**

blunt, non-retractile claws **29**

29 1 molar in upper jaw behind the carnassial . . . .
Family: **Hyaenidae**

3 molars in upper jaw behind the carnassial . . . .
Family: **Canidae**

30 body covered with spines . . . .
Family: **Erinaceidae**

body not covered with spines. **31**

31 forelimbs short, with spade-shaped extremities . . . .
    Family: **Talpidae**

    forelimbs without spade-shaped extremities **32**

32 hindlegs greatly elongated, eyes very large. . . . .
    Family: **Macroscelididae**

    hindlegs not elongated, eyes very small. . . . . . .
    Family: **Soricidae**

33 all 4 limbs clearly discernible, in the form of flippers. **34**
    Order: Pinnipedia

    hindlimbs absent, horizontal flukes at the end of the body **35**
    Order: Cetacea

34 hindlimbs dragged behind the body . . . .
    Family: **Phocidae**

    hindlimbs turned forward . . . .
    Family: **Odobaenidae**

35 toothless jaws; long, triangular bony plates
    hanging from upper jaw into mouth cavity **36**

    toothed jaws, or at least toothed lower jaw. **37**

36 very large head, pectoral fins (flippers)
    rounded, dorsal fin absent, neck smooth . . . .
    Family: **Balaenidae**

    head smaller, flatter, flippers pointed,
    dorsal fin present, neck grooved . . . .
    Family: **Balaenopteridae**

37 forehead blunt, teeth in lower jaw only . . . .
    Family: **Physeteridae**

    forehead rounded or tapering to a long point, both jaws toothed **38**

38 dorsal fin absent. . . . .
    Family: **Monodontidae**

    dorsal fin triangular in shape . . . .
    Family: **Delphinidae**

Guide to species

Key to measurement abbreviations

general:

Lhb	—	length of head and body
Lt	—	length of tail
Lhp	—	length of underside of hindpaw
H	—	height at shoulder
W	—	weight

bats only:

Lf	—	length of forearm
Lth	—	length of thumb
Wsp	—	wingspan

hares only: **Le**   — length of ear

seals, whales
and dolphins: **L**   — total body length

European Hedgehog
Erinaceus europaeus

Order: Insectivora
Family: Erinaceidae

Hedgehogs are easily recognizable by their spiny backs. They come out at dusk or at night, mostly spending the daytime in nests of grass and leaves concealed in vegetation, among stones or below stumps. Their poor flight reactions considerably increase the likelihood of meeting them but unfortunately, this is also the reason so many are killed on the roads. Hedgehogs of temperate and cold climatic zones pass the winter in hibernation; this lasts in central Europe from October till April, in the British Isles from the end of November or the beginning of December until March. During hibernation their metabolism slows down, body temperature dropping as low as 4 °C. The female usually has two litters each year, each litter containing 4—6 young. The gestation period is 5—6 weeks. The young are born blind and naked, after a few days soft spines start developing on their backs (2). They leave the nest at 3 weeks and follow their mother for another fortnight or so. When in danger, hedgehogs curl up into a spiny ball — this is achieved through circular muscles situated below the skin all over the body (3). Hedgehogs feed on various species of insects, snails, worms and occasionally take bird's eggs and young from nests or some plant food.

The European Hedgehog (1) is found throughout the Britisch Isles. At elevations above 450 m in Scotland it occurs less frequently, and it was probably introduced to Ireland and some other islands. On the continent it ranges eastward to Norway, Sweden, Finland, and to the northwestern parts of the former USSR. In central Europe it meets the Eastern Hedgehog (*E. concolor*) (4). The two species share a 200-km wide zone along a line stretching from the Baltic to the Adriatic. The European Hedgehog is a typical inhabitant of European woodlands, and deciduous and mixed forest is its favourite habitat. It is very adaptable, however, and is also found in open country, hedgerows, parks, and gardens. The prints of both fore- (6) and hindfeet (7) show the entire sole with five long toes armed with narrow claws.

The Eastern Hedgehog is originally native to the steppes and forested plains, and avoids continuous forest cover. It colonizes cultivated land, and the warmer and drier sites in open country. Both species are also found in villages and towns. The Algerian or Vagrant Hedgehog (*Aethechinus algirus*) (5) inhabits north Africa, the Canary Islands, the Balearic Islands, Spain, and both southeastern and southwestern France. The Long-eared Hedgehog (*Hemiechinus auritus*) is found from northern Libya and Egypt to Asia Minor and on Cyprus. Its European distribution is confined to steppes in the Volga and Don basins.

The folk-lore that hedgehogs are immune to snake venom is false, although they do appear to tolerate larger doses of venom than other animals of equal size. The spines on their heads successfully repel any snake that tries to attack them, and hedgehogs are surprisingly quick to bite the snake's spine in two, having overcome it without being bitten themselves. Unfortunately, there is no truth either in the fable that hedgehogs pick up apples and pears on their spines and carry them to their burrow.

	Lhb (mm)	Lt (mm)	W (g)
Erinaceus europaeus	225—295	20—35	500—1,200
E. concolor	226—295	20—35	500—850
Aethechinus algirus	200—250	20—40	400—850
Hemiechinus auritus	225—300	20—40	550—1,200

Common Shrew
Sorex araneus

Order: Insectivora
Family: Soricidae

Shrews are commonly confused with mice, but even a cursory glance at the long, highly mobile snout equipped with tactile whiskers and projecting beyond the incisors will prevent the mistake. Shrews have a keen sense of hearing and touch, but their sight is weak. The fur is dense and short, almost entirely covering the outer ear. The scent glands located on the sides of the body play an important role during the breeding season in communication between partners and in marking territories. All shrew species are very similar and for exact identification it is therefore often necessary to examine their teeth and compare their body measurements. Shrews do not hibernate and forage for food even under snow. They are active during the day and the night, periods of intense activity regularly alternating with short periods of sleep spent in burrows or in nests under the bark of trees, in stumps or in tufts of grass. They often produce squeaking and twittering sounds which betray their otherwise well-concealed presence. Some species emit high-frequency sound and orientate themselves in the darkness just like bats. Their diet consists of insects, worms, slugs, and occasionally small vertebrates. The females produce 2—4 litters a year; spring litters usually have larger numbers of young than autumn ones. The gestation period is 19—21 days but in females already suckling it is prolonged to 27 days, so that a female always suckles a single litter at a time. Shrews are short-lived: they live to about 1 1/2 years old and usually die of old age in the summer of the year after they were born.

Shrews of the genus *Sorex* have 32 teeth with reddish brown tips (2, *S. araneus*; 3, *S. alpinus*; 4, *S. minutus*). The biology of all the species in the genus is very similar. They favour relatively damp habitats and densely overgrown sites; in the mountains some species may be found up to the timberline.

The Common Shrew (1) is found throughout Europe with the exception of Iceland, Ireland, the Iberian Peninsula and the Mediterranean islands, and its range extends as far as central Siberia. It is abundant in mainland Britain, and is found on most of the islands around the coast except for the Scilly Isles, Lundy, the Isle of Man, the Outer Hebrides and the Shetlands. Though characteristically a woodland animal, it can also be found in fields and gardens and finds its way into buildings. The Alpine Shrew (*S. alpinus*) (5) is confined to the mountains of central Europe, to the Alps, Carpathians, Pyrenees, and the Balkan Peninsula. The distribution of the Pygmy Shrew (*S. minutus*) (6) roughly coincides with that of the Common Shrew, and the two species often live side by side. The Pygmy Shrew is quite plentiful in the British Isles and is the only shrew found in Ireland, but has not been reported from the Scilly Isles, Shetland and the Channel Islands. It is only rarely encountered outside woodland. The Least Shrew (*S. minutissimus*) (7) inhabits the spruce forests covering the tundra of northern Europe and Asia as far east as Japan, tending to favour drier localities. The Masked or Laxmann's Shrew (*S. caecutiens*) (8) occurs in similar habitats, reaching as far as the taiga. It ranges from Scandinavia over Siberia to Sakhalin and Japan, and also makes its appearance as a relict species (e.g. in northern Poland). Shrews are difficult to catch and breed in captivity. In traps they soon starve and lose heat as their metabolism is extraordinarily rapid. The amount of food consumed by a shrew in a day often exceeds its body weight. They are also delicate in other respects: in unusual situations, as when picked up in the hand, shrews can die on the spot of nervous shock.

	Lhb (mm)	Lt (mm)	W (g)
Sorex araneus	55—85	34—50	5.5—14
S. alpinus	60—75	60—75	6.5—12
S. minutus	40—60	30—45	2.5—7
S. minutissimus	33—45	23—29	1.8—4
S. caecutiens	48—70	30—45	3—8

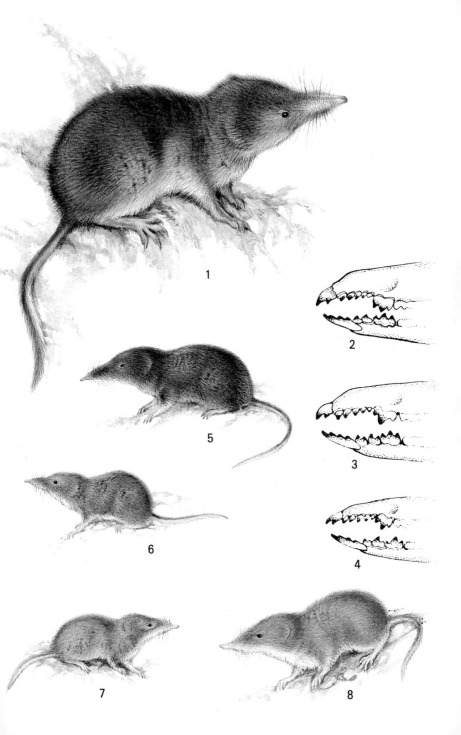

Water Shrew
Neomys fodiens

Order: Insectivora
Family: Soricidae

Shrews of the genus *Neomys* also have teeth with red-brown tips; there are, however, only four instead of five single-pointed teeth in the upper jaw. The total number of teeth in the dentition is 30 (2, *N. fodiens*; 3, *N. anomalus*) compared with the 32 of the genus *Sorex*. The Water Shrew (1) is found in England, Scotland and Wales and on some of the islands, but not in Ireland. On the Continent it is absent from Spain and Turkey. There are isolated populations by the Amur estuary and on the island of Sakhalin. Its favourite habitat is overgrown banks beside still or running water. It may also be found in damp places far from water, in forests and meadows. It is a good swimmer (4) and diver, capable of remaining under water for 20 seconds or more. The Water Shrew is excellently adapted for aquatic life, the underside of its tail being equipped with a keel of stiff bristles which serve as a rudder; similar bristles extend the surface of its hindpaws and help in paddling (7). When swimming it uses all four limbs and makes running movements. The Water Shrew is active by day and night, foraging for food mainly in water but also on dry land. It lives on insects and their larvae, crustaceans, molluscs, frogs and small fish, storing the surplus for later use. It stays in the water only for short intervals, on land often grooming its thick, fine fur, spreading the secretions from sebaceous glands. When diving, masses of tiny air bubbles remain trapped in the fur, insulating the animal and giving it the appearance of a small silvery cylinder. The Water Shrew digs burrows in banks; these are oval in cross-section and usually have one underwater entrance. The female gives birth to her young in the subterranean nest. Between April and October, after a pregnancy of 24 days, she usually produces two litters of 5—9 young which she suckles for 37 days. She has five pairs of nipples. The Water Shrew's upperparts are almost always black, the underparts may be white, rusty-yellow (5) or blackish.

The Mediterranean Water Shrew (*N. anomalus*) (6) is also characterized by black-and-white colouring, frequently with a silvery hue. Isolated populations of this species occur in central Europe, in Spain and in the Balkans, reaching to the southern parts of the former USSR. Being less dependent on water than *N. fodiens*, it is more commonly found in swamps and on wet ground. Its excursions into the water are less frequent, the bristles fringing the underside of the tail and the hindpaws are less well-developed. It is also less likely to dig its own burrows and tunnels. In winter it may occasionally be caught in houses. It eats chiefly insects, molluscs and worms. As it is a relatively rare and retiring animal, little is known about its reproduction, but in all probability it is not very different from that of the Water Shrew. It is assumed that there are 3–11 young in each litter. The female usually has six pairs of nipples. Like the other members of the shrew family, the two species discussed here possess scent glands on their flanks which emit a strong musky odour, particularly in the breeding season. This is why carnivores often leave shrews they have caught without eating them. It has even been asserted that, at various times, their flesh is poisonous. The secretion of a gland beneath the lower jaw in the Water Shrew does indeed contain a substance of similar chemical composition to cobra venom. It is not known whether the similar glands of the Mediterranean Water Shrew contain a similar poison.

	Lhb (mm)	Lt (mm)	Lhp (mm)	W (g)
Neomys fodiens	70—90	60—70	18—21	10.5—20
N. anomalus	65—90	45—61	15—17	13—20

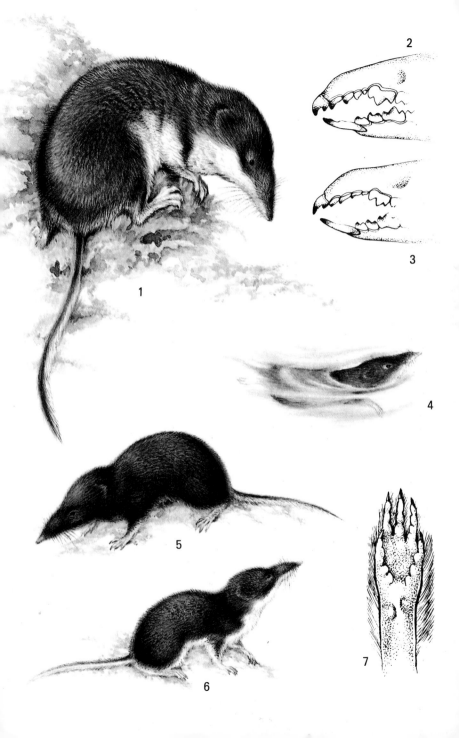

Bicoloured White-toothed Shrew

Crocidura leucodon

Order: Insectivora
Family: Soricidae

Shrews of the genera *Crocidura* and *Suncus* possess completely white teeth lacking brown tips. In the genus *Crocidura* there are three single-pointed teeth in the upper jaw (2, *C. leucodon*; 3, *C. suaveolens*; 4, *C. russula*), while in the genus *Suncus* there are four. Long hairs protrude sideways from the flattened fur covering the tail. The ears are larger than in other shrews, and jut conspicuously out of the fur. These shrews are warmth-loving and are widespread in the warmer regions of Europe, Africa and southern Asia. They are much less aggressive than other shrews and individuals tolerate each other even when assembled in large numbers. Species inhabiting colder regions take to human dwellings and woodstacks for the winter. The Bicoloured White-toothed Shrew (1) is found throughout southern and central Europe but is absent from southern France, Spain, southern Italy, and the western part of the Balkan Peninsula. It ranges eastward across Asia Minor to central Siberia, avoiding continuous forest and mountains. Its typical habitats are the warm and dry steppes and open country. It favours terrain overgrown with low, sparse vegetation and may also be found in fields. It is an adept climber. The female usually produces two litters of 3—9 young in the period from April to September. The gestation period lasts 31—33 days. The nest is built of grass and leaves stuck together with mud.

The Lesser White-toothed or Scilly Shrew (*C. suaveolens*) (5) ranges from Spain over central and southern Europe and north Africa, to Asia Minor and to the southern parts of the former USSR. Its presence in the British Isles is restricted to the Scilly Isles, Jersey and Sark. In the northernmost parts of its range it lives chiefly in buildings. Although it prefers warm open habitats it can be encountered in mountain woods up to elevations of 1,000 m. Its reproduction is similar to that of *C. leucodon*; the gestation period is 26–27 days, the number of young in a litter mostly 4–5. The Common European White-toothed Shrew (*C. russula*) (6) is an inhabitant of western Europe reaching eastward to Saxony, in the British Isles it is confined to Alderney, Guernsey and Herm in the Channel Islands. It also occurs in the Near East, in north Africa, throughout temperate Asia, and in Africa as far south as Angola. Compared with the species described above it favours damper habitats with dense vegetation, gardens, woodland edges and valleys. The breeding period extends from February to November, otherwise its biology is similar to that of *C. leucodon*. Since in the wild it sometimes survives a second winter, its life span is longer than that of other shrews.

The Etruscan or Savi's Pygmy Shrew (*Suncus etruscus*) (7) is, with the Least Shrew (*Sorex minutissimus*), one of the smallest mammals in the world. It occurs in southern Europe, the Near East and north Africa, and also in southern Asia and in eastern and southern Africa. This small shrew is most commonly found in gardens and fields near human dwellings, but also in sparsely populated woodlands where the soil is not too wet. Its diet consists mainly of spiders and small insects. In cool periods or when food is short the Etruscan Shrew becomes torpid and its body temperature drops. It may remain in this condition for several hours, with a rise in temperature it becomes active again. It usually produces 5—6 litters a year, gestation lasts approximately 28 days, and there are normally 4 young in a litter.

When outside the nest, females of all species of white-toothed shrews lead their young in file: each holds with its teeth the base of the tail of the one in front, forming a 'caravan' (8).

	Lhb (mm)	Lt (mm)	W (g)
Crocidura leucodon	65—85	30—40	7—13
C. suaveolens	55—78	30—43	6—9.50
C. russula	65—95	35—50	6—14
S. etruscus	35—45	25—28	1.5—2

Russian Desman
Desmana moschata

Order: Insectivora
Family: Talpidae

Desmans are unusual amongst insectivores in being excellently adapted for life in water. Their hindfeet are much larger than the forefeet, are webbed, and are fringed with bristly hairs which expand the surface area of the paw. Using its long, extremely mobile snout, a desman can take a breath without emerging above the surface. The fur is thick, with a metallic sheen. Immediately under the base of the tail there is a gland exuding a strong musky secretion.

The Russian Desman (1) lives in the lower Volga, Don and Ural basins, and in the Mius and Sambek rivers which empty into the Sea of Azov. Although it is diurnal, it is rarely seen for it spends the greater part of its waking hours in water or in a burrow. The favourite habitats are the calm, vegetation-filled waters of river bends and oxbow lakes no more than 1—2 m deep. Temporary burrows are simple and short, a permanent nest burrow may be up to 10 m long, ending in a spacious nest chamber lined with grass and leaves (3), and may be shared by four or five desmans. The Russian Desman breeds twice a year, in spring and autumn. Pregnancy lasts 45—50 days and a litter consists of 1—5 young. It eats aquatic snails, leeches, insects, and—chiefly in winter—some plant food. It used to be hunted for the splendid fur which was sold as 'silver muskrat', but since 1920 hunting has been prohibited.

The Pyrenean Desman (*Galemys pyrenaicus*) (2) is found in northern Portugal, Spain and southwestern France. It lives chiefly in mountain streams at 300—1,200 m, but may also appear in marshes with streams running through them. In contrast to the Russian Desman, this is a nocturnal animal which searches for food on land as well as in the water. Insects and their larvae make up the greater part of its diet. The mating season lasts from January to June and the young are usually born after a gestation period of around 50 days. There are usually 4 young in each litter.

The North-African Elephant Shrew (*Elephantulus roseti*) (4) is a representative of an exclusively African family of insectivores, the elephant shrews (Macrosceliti-dae). It is widespread in the semi-desert regions of northwestern Africa, from southwestern Morocco to western Libya. Elephant shrews, though normally going on all four legs, move rapidly by jumping along on their long hindlegs just like kangaroos, for example when danger threatens. They are diurnal and live either singly or in pairs. Various insects, such as ants, beetles and locusts make up their diet, and they never drink, obtaining all the water they need from their food. After an eight-week pregnancy the female gives birth to two young, which reach maturity in only 5 weeks. As a rule, the female produces no more than three litters throughout her life.

	Lhb (mm)	Lt (mm)	W (g)
Desmana moschata	180—215	170—220	300—400
Galemys pyrenaicus	110—135	130—155	50—80
Elephantulus roseti	130—140	110—115	70—130

Common Mole

Talpa europaea

Order: Insectivora
Family: Talpidae

The first sign of a mole's presence is usually the molehills thrown up on the surface of a field or lawn as it digs its burrows. Moles are insectivores and are exceptionally well adapted for their underground life. The fur is very short and thick, the eyes are small or completely covered with skin, external ears are missing, and the tail is short. The strong, spade-shaped forelimbs, with palms facing outward, are ideally adapted for digging. Individual species are difficult to distinguish by external characteristics alone, for even their size is very variable, depending on climate, food supply and other environmental factors. They are best distinguished by skeletal characteristics, especially the nasal part of the skull (2, *T. caeca*; 3, *T. europaea*; 4, *T. romana*) and the teeth.

The Common Mole (1) is abundant in mainland Britain and on Anglesey, Mull, Skye, the Isle of Wight, Alderney and Jersey, but is not found in Ireland. Its northern range extends across southern Sweden eastwards as far as the river Ob, and in the south it is found from Spain over northern Italy and the northern Balkan Peninsula to the Caucasus and the Caspian Sea. The Mediterranean or Blind Mole (*T. caeca*) (5) inhabits the Iberian Peninsula, southern France and northern Italy, from where it ranges along the Adriatic coast throughout the southern part of the Balkan Peninsula, and through the Near East as far as the Caucasus. The Roman Mole (*T. romana*) lives in southern Italy and Sicily and in mountains on the Balkan Peninsula.

The biology of the three species mentioned is almost identical. Most of their life is spent underground in their burrows. The nest lies hidden under a large molehill, usually connected to a concentric system of runways (6). Moles are strictly solitary, each tunnel system being inhabited by a single individual. In the breeding period pairs remain together for a short time, and females stay with their young for 4—5 weeks while suckling. Moles are active throughout the day and night. Active periods last approximately 4^1/$_2$ hours, interspersed with rest periods of around 3^1/$_2$ hours. The rutting season is brief, lasting from the end of February until May. The female usually produces one and rarely two litters of 4—6 young a year. Gestation lasts 28—42 days. The mole's life span is 3—4 years, and males attain sexual maturity in their second season.

Their diet is chiefly earthworms but they also take insects and gastropods. Moles will also eat small vertebrates which they come across in the tunnels. When food is plentiful, moles often gather supplies for use in the near future. They paralyse earthworms by biting the 'head' end and deposit them in a 'store-chamber'. Moles mostly occur in loose soil, in meadows, pastures, arable fields and gardens, and also in deciduous forests. Tunnels are 20—40 cm below the surface, depending on the type of soil, and in winter moles burrow deeper. After leaving the nest, the young usually dig shallower tunnels and are therefore more often encountered above ground.

In some parts of their range, for example in the former USSR, moles are usually hunted for their fur.

	Lhb (mm)	Lt (mm)	Lhp (mm)	W (g)	Eyes
Talpa europaea	125—150	30—40	17—20.5	60—115	Visible
T. caeca	100—130	22—40	14—18	30—65	Covered with skin
T. romana	110—140	26—36	17—19	65—120	Covered with skin

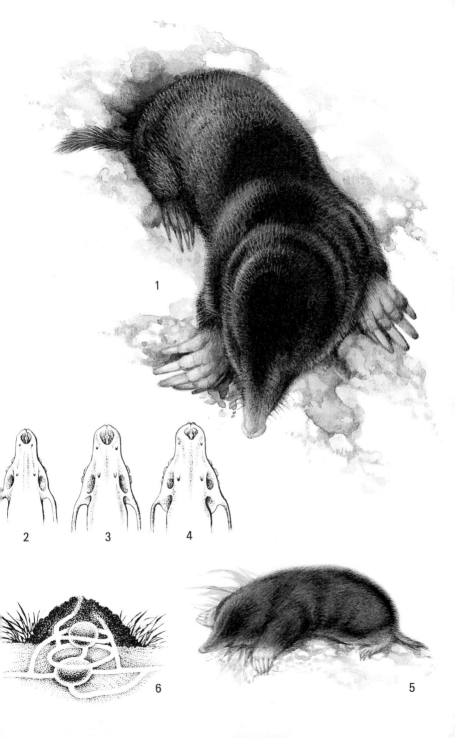

1

2   3   4

6   5

Greater Horseshoe Bat
Rhinolophus ferrumequinum

Order: Chiroptera
Family: Rhinolophidae

Horseshoe bats (Rhinolophidae) differ from evening bats (Vespertilionidae) in having a conspicuous horseshoe-shaped membranous outgrowth on the nose. These membranes are involved in echolocation, by which horseshoe bats orientate themselves in the darkness. Moving their heads, they send out through the nostrils a directed stream of signals at a frequency of 80—100 kHz. Each signal lasts approximately one-tenth of a second, which means that sound reflected by objects nearer than 15 m returns before the sound itself has died away. In this way the bat 'feels' the space around it. The horseshoe membranes vary from species to species and are essential identifying features (2, *R. ferrumequinum*; 3, *R. hipposideros*). Horseshoe bats can detect far more delicate obstacles than can evening bats. They fly low, on their broad, rounded wings, with a flapping flight. Characteristic of horseshoe bats are a pair of false nipples located low on the female's abdomen. Before they are able to fly, the young cling to these nipples while their mother is on the wing, sometimes even when at rest. Horseshoe bats never hide in crevices but always hang freely from cave ceilings, clinging with their feet, and enveloped in their wings.

All the species have a similar biology. In summer they often assemble in large colonies in caves or in lofts (this particularly applies to the Lesser Horseshoe Bat), in winter they gather in caves or tunnels where the temperature remains steady at around 6—10 °C. Mating usually takes place in September and October before hibernation. The live sperm are stored in the female until spring when ovulation and fertilization take place. Two or three months later one, rarely two, young are born. Horseshoe bats feed on nocturnal insects. Their life span is relatively long, the average age being 3—5 years, but an age of 18 years has been recorded in the Lesser Horseshoe and 26 years in the Greater Horseshoe.

The Greater Horseshoe Bat (1) is found throughout southern and western Europe, North Africa and Asia Minor, throughout Asia to China and Japan. In the British Isles it occurs chiefly in western and southern England, and in south and west Wales. In central Europe, isolated populations occur where the climate allows.

The Lesser Horseshoe Bat (*R. hipposideros*) (4) lives in western Ireland, Wales, southwestern England, and the Midlands. In continental Europe it is common up to about latitude 52 °N, and may also be found in north Africa and south-western Asia. It likes hunting grounds with thin tree cover. The Mediterranean Horseshoe Bat (*R. euryale*) (5) is an inhabitant of southern Europe, north Africa and southwestern Asia. It lives all the year round in caves and other subterranean spaces. Unlike other horseshoe bats, the Mediterranean Horseshoe Bats, when hanging, are never completely wrapped in their wings. Blasius' Horseshoe Bat (*R. blasii*) (6) occurs in Italy, along the eastern Adriatic coast as far as Greece, on Cyprus, in the Near East and north Africa, extending southward as far as southern Africa.

In Europe, a rapid decline in the numbers of horseshoe bats has recently been recorded. This is due on the one hand to the destruction of their habitats and interference with their hibernation sites, and on the other hand, to the decreasing numbers of insects as a result of the widespread use of insecticides. Horseshoe bats are now among the most endangered European mammals.

	Lhb (mm)	Lf (mm)	Wsp (mm)	W (g)
Rhinolophus				
ferrumequinum	56—75	50—61	330—385	16—28
R. hipposideros	40—45	34—41	228—250	3.5—10
R. euryale	43—58	43—50	250—300	10—17.5
R. blasii	44—56	45—48	330—400	10—18

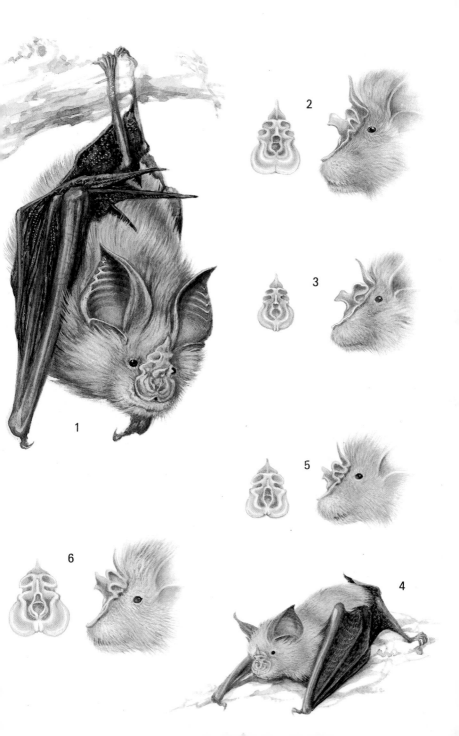

Large Mouse-eared Bat

Order: Chiroptera

Myotis myotis

Family: Vespertilionidae

The family of evening bats (Vespertilionidae) is very numerous indeed and is the most widespread of all the Chiroptera. Unlike horseshoe bats, evening bats have no membranous outgrowth on the nose, having instead a membranous projection in the ear—the tragus or lid. Short echolocation signals are emitted through the mouth, and are frequency modulated during transmission. Evening bats live in caves, in buildings and also holes in the trunks of trees, forming winter and summer colonies. They can crawl on walls and on the ground. When hibernating they do not wrap their wings around themselves (8). For the most part they catch their food—nocturnal insects—in the air; some species, however, can also take beetles and other insects from trees and from the ground. All evening bats drink regularly, usually while flying close to the surface of the water.

The Large Mouse-eared Bat (1, 2) is common all over continental Europe and eastwards to the Near East. In Britain it was first recorded in 1888 at Girton near Cambridge; more recently, several individuals have been caught in Dorset and Sussex. It prefers open land, avoiding large areas of forest and the larger towns. Summer colonies usually live in lofts. These colonies are formed by females and young only, males living singly at this time of the year. In the autumn, both sexes gather in caves. Mating takes place at the end of summer and in the autumn, but the sperm remain inactive and fertilization is delayed until the female reawakens from hibernation. There is usually only a single young. The duration of pregnancy depends on the temperature prevailing in the roost. When the female leaves for a foraging flight, the young remain hidden in the roost.

The Whiskered Bat (*M. mystacinus*) (3) is found throughout Europe and Asia to Japan and Indonesia, and is also found in northwestern Africa. In Britain it is restricted to isolated areas in England, the Welsh borders, and Scotland. It is a forest dweller, preferring a relatively humid climate. In summer it stays in trees and lofts. It hibernates in caves, but never in large numbers.

Brandt's Bat (*M. brandti*) (6) is very similar and the two species are not easily distinguished in the wild. They have to be identified by distinguishing features present, for example, on the skull or on the teeth (4, *M. brandti*; 5, *M. mystacinus*). Their distribution and biology are similar, but in Britain *M. brandti* is uncommon and confined to southern counties.

Daubenton's Bat or Water Bat (*M. daubentoni*) (7) ranges from western Europe as far as eastern Asia, but is rare in some parts of southern Europe. There are isolated populations in England, North Wales, Scotland and eastern Ireland. Woods with plenty of hollow trees and near to water are its favourite habitats, for it mostly hunts over water for gnats and caddis flies. Like other bats it mates in the autumn, and also during the hibernation period. Towards the end of June a single young is born.

Members of the genus *Myotis* live in different habitats in summer and winter. (The only exceptions are species of warm regions which live in caves all the year round.) The same hibernating sites, especially old mining galleries and caves, are often used by the local population over several hundred years and bats often assemble there in great numbers. Any interference with hibernating bats endangers their life for if they are roused from sleep, their metabolism accelerates and the fat reserves needed to survive the winter are rapidly consumed. Safeguarding bats' hibernating sites is one of the most important factors in their protection.

	Lhb (mm)	Lf (mm)	Wsp (mm)	W (g)
Myotis myotis	70—83	56—67	368—394	18—45
M. mystacinus	35—48	30—37	225—245	3.1—6.6
M. brandti	40—51	32—38	200—230	4.3—8.3
M. daubentoni	36—60	33—40	220—245	6.5—10

Common Pipistrelle
Pipistrellus pipistrellus

Order: Chiroptera
Family: Vespertilionidae

The genus *Pipistrellus* is widely distributed in both the Old and the New World. Pipistrelles are small, with rounded ears and a short, rounded tragus, a membranous outgrowth in the ear. The various species are very similar and can often only be identified by their teeth (2, *P. pipistrellus*; 3, *P. kuhli*).

The Common Pipistrelle (1) is found in Europe, Asia and north Africa, and is the most common bat in some parts of Europe. It is very common in the British Isles, and is the most common species in Ireland. In summer the Common Pipistrelle forms large colonies in buildings, and occasionally is found in hollow trees. It has a predilection for crevices, liking to hide between beams, in roofs, and behind picture frames in churches for example. At the annual migration, usually in August and September, it often appears in large numbers in the most unusual places, coming into houses where it hides behind picture frames, in windows, in lamps and other confined spaces. This invasion occurs as the summer colony disintegrates but no real explanation for it has yet been found. In the southern parts of its range this bat hibernates in caves, while northern populations commonly spend the winter in crevices in walls, church towers and so on.

Kuhl's Pipistrelle (*P. kuhli*) (4) inhabits southern Europe and Asia as far as Pakistan, in Africa it ranges from the Mediterranean to Cape Province, avoiding the virgin rainforest. It is one of the few easily identifiable species, as the back edge of its wing is rimmed with white.

Savi's Pipistrelle (*P. savii*) (5) lives in southern Europe, Asia and northwestern Africa. It likes rocky areas, being found above the timberline in the mountains; in the Alps it has been found at over 2,000 m.

Nathusius' Pipistrelle (*P. nathusii*) (6) ranges across Europe, reaching as far as the Urals and the Caucasus; in western Europe, however, there are only isolated populations. In Britain it was discovered in Dorset as late as 1969. It typically lives in deciduous forests near water. It spends most of the year in holes in trunks and crevices in buildings. Nathusius' Pipistrelle is a migratory species frequently covering very long distances to reach its wintering sites: populations from central Russia fly 600—1,600 km to the Balkans and Turkey.

The biology of all pipistrelles is similar. They fly at moderate heights with a rapid, jerky flight, turning frequently. Half an hour or so after sunset they leave the roost to hunt small insects, especially gnats. They go into hibernation relatively late, in central Europe often not before December. If you catch sight of a bat flying outdoors on a warm winter day, it is almost sure to be a pipistrelle. Female pipistrelles usually produce two young. The life span of these small animals can be surprisingly long, up to 15 years, with an average age of 3 years.

	Lhb (mm)	Lf (mm)	Wsp (mm)	W (g)
Pipistrellus pipistrellus	32—52	27—34	200—235	3—8
P. kuhli	40—47	32—35	220—232	5—8.5
P. savii	43—48	32—38	230—245	5.2—10
P. nathusii	40—58	31—35	230—245	5—9

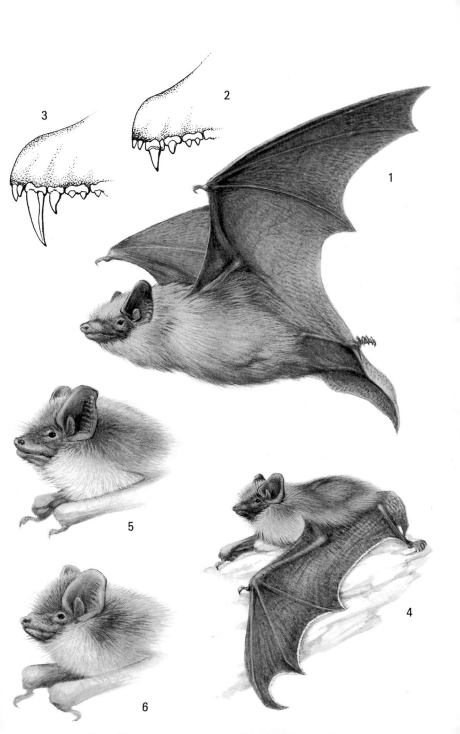

Noctule Bat or Common Noctule
Nyctalus noctula

Order: Chiroptera
Family: Vespertilionidae

Bats of the genus *Nyctalus* live in old hollow trees in summer, and are primarily forest-dwellers. The Noctule Bat (1) is widespread throughout Europe and Asia as far as Burma. It is relatively common in England, especially in the southeast, is sporadic in Wales and has been reported in Scotland on a few occasions. Where man has transformed forests into cultivated land, this species has adapted itself relatively well and may be found (especially at the time of migration flights) in buildings, in crevices between stones and in air-shafts. It leaves the roost in the late afternoon or early evening to hunt for insects, flying rapidly above the trees. It can be identified by its narrow wings and long tail (2). The Noctule Bat is a gregarious species. Summer colonies usually comprise 20—100 individuals, winter colonies about 600. Summer colonies occupy large hollow trees, often beside ponds. The edge of the entrance is usually blackened, and the bark below is marked with a dark band of urine and droppings. Swarms of flies buzz around the opening. Loud squeakings can be heard from far off, especially on a warm afternoon. In the autumn Noctule Bats occasionally assemble in small mating groups of 2—7 individuals. Little is known about their hibernation sites, as these are in the underground reaches of hollow trees, rock crevices and inaccessible spaces within buildings. In June the female usually gives birth to two young which often attain maturity the same year.

The Giant Noctule (*N. lasiopterus*) (3) resembles the Noctule but is much larger. It is rare and there is little information on its distribution. It has been found in southern Europe, Switzerland, the Balkans, Turkey and north Africa but not in Britain. The northern limit of its range probably extends from southern Poland to the Urals.

Leisler's Bat or Lesser Noctule (*N. leisleri*) (4) is found from Ireland and Portugal eastwards to the Near East, and also in the Azores and Madeira. It is common in Ireland, and has been occasionally found in Essex, Herefordshire, Kent and Yorkshire, and once in the Shetland Islands. On the Azores it is mostly active during the day. Its general behaviour is similar to that of the Common Noctule but there is usually only a single young.

The Serotine Bat (*Eptesicus serotinus*) (5) is quite common throughout Europe and Asia as well as in North Africa. In the British Isles it is found mainly in the southeast and occasionally in Dorset and Somerset, often making an appearance in towns. It starts hunting in the early evening, flying low to catch beetles and moths, and sometimes settling on trees to pick insects off the branches. Summer colonies usually consist of 10—50 individuals and inhabit lofts and other indoor spaces. During June, a single young is born. In winter Serotines are rarely encountered underground: they prefer to hibernate in crevices in buildings and rock faces.

The Northern Bat (*E. nilssoni*) ranges from eastern France and Norway eastward to the Pacific Ocean. It is the only bat to penetrate beyond the Arctic Circle, southwards it mostly lives in mountains frequently up to a height of 2,000 m. It especially likes alpine coniferous and mixed forests, and is usually seen just after sunset hunting near water and in damp places in the forest.

	Lhb (mm)	Lf (mm)	Wsp (mm)	W (g)
Nyctalus noctula	65—84	46—55	353—387	20—40
N. lasiopterus	78—104	62—69	410—450	41—76
N. leisleri	53—66	35—46	290—320	12—20
Eptesicus serotinus	62—80	48—57	348—380	13—32
E. nilssoni	45—54	37—46	240—270	8—13

1

2

3

4

5

Long-eared Bat
Plecotus auritus

Order: Chiroptera
Family: Vespertilionidae

Bats of the genus *Plecotus* are easily distinguished by their huge ears whose edges come together on the forehead. During hibernation the ears are under the wings, leaving only the tragi jutting out.

The Long-eared Bat (1, 2) is found throughout most of Europe and northern Asia. It is widespread in mainland Britain and Ireland, in its favourite habitat of damp woodland. In summer it lives in hollow trees, nest-boxes, and buildings; in winter it seeks refuge underground in caves, mines and cellars. With a slow fluttering flight it hunts mostly moths and butterflies, less frequently beetles and flies, often picking insects from leaves or branches while hovering on the spot. It also hovers above water to drink. It never starts hunting before dusk, and usually eats its prey in concealment. A single young is born in June or July. As with the other evening bats (Vespertilionidae), the mother leaves it hanging on a wall or ceiling (3) while she feeds and returns only to suckle it. The young are fully developed in about a month but generally do not attain sexual maturity before their second year. Females usually form small summer colonies, while males are sometimes solitary. There are no large winter colonies but small clusters of individuals are often found, hibernating in buildings. The ears have special cross-wise muscles which enable the bat to fold them like an accordion when at rest. Large glands are situated on both sides of the relatively broad snout; these emit a strong smelling oily secretion, particularly at the time of migration flights. The bats spread it over their fur and use it for marking their roosts.

The Grey Long-eared Bat (*P. austriacus*) (4) closely resembles the Long-eared Bat and, until fairly recently, they were not recognized as separate species (the differences are shown in 5). The best diagnostic feature is the wingspan: in *P. auritus* males it is less than 265 mm, in females 270 mm; in *P. austriacus* males it is over 265 mm, in females over 270 mm. In most of their range the two species live side by side, but the Grey Long-eared Bat has a more southerly distribution extending to Africa as far as Senegal, and to the Near East and central Asia. A rare find was reported in 1875 from Hampshire and a colony was discovered in Dorset in 1964. Its favourite hiding places are rock fissures, small caves, and buildings. It spends the winter in underground hiding places, often hanging freely on walls and not hidden in crevices. Its reproduction and behaviour are almost identical with the Long-eared Bat.

Bats of the genus *Plecotus* do not migrate long distances. Towards the end of March or at the beginning of April, they awaken from hibernation and move to their summer habitats. They return to their winter roosts as late as the end of October or the beginning of November. In August and September, at the time the summer colonies break up, young individuals may also invade houses, like pipistrelles. Both the Long-eared Bat and the Grey Long-eared Bat are extremely sensitive to any kind of disturbance. When alarmed, the colony usually moves to another hiding place which may be several kilometres away.

	Lhb (mm)	Lf (mm)	Lth (mm)	W (g)
Plecotus auritus	40—50	34—42	over 6	5—10
P. austriacus	41—60	37—43	under 6	5—12

Barbastelle
Barbastella barbastellus

Order: Chiroptera
Family: Vespertilionidae

The Barbastelle (1) cannot be confused with any other species. The short snout and ears connecting on the forehead lend its face the characteristic expression of a tiny pug dog. It is found in western, central and southern Europe and Morocco. In Britain it is found mainly in southern England, with isolated finds reported from Yorkshire, Carlisle and Wales. In Asia Minor and central Asia it is replaced by the dark brown, very similar species *B. leucomelas*. In central Europe it is common but is mostly known from its underground hibernation sites, where colonies of many hundred individuals can often be found. These colonies are composed chiefly of males and it is assumed that females probably hibernate elsewhere, maybe in hollow trees or rock crevices. The Barbastelle, being very hardy, goes into hibernation as late as December. It hibernates at temperatures of 0—5 °C and usually leaves its winter roost in March. In summer it is solitary, being found in crevices in hollow trees, in thatched roofs or behind shutters. It hunts small moths, beetles and flies. The female usually bears a single young.

Schreiber's Bat (*Miniopterus schreibersi*) (2,3) is another distinctive species with a short snout, a domed head and arched brow, and ears almost concealed in the fur which, on the head, is almost velvety and quite different from the fur on the rest of the body. The second phalanx of the third wing toe is almost three times as long as the first phalanx of the same toe, while in the other evening bats it is never more than twice as long. Schreiber's Bat is found in isolated colonies throughout southern Europe; its northern limit passes through southern France, Bavaria and Austria. It is a cave-dweller forming large colonies and flying long distances, often more than 200 km. Soon after dusk it leaves the roost and flies rapidly, hunting mostly moths. Mating takes place in autumn, but unlike other bats, the egg is fertilized immediately; a latent period sets in during which the embryo stops developing. The single young (rarely two) is born in June or July, as with other species.

Another remarkable species is the European Free-tailed Bat (*Tadarida teniotis*) (4). It is a member of the family Molossidae which is particularly widespread in the tropical regions of both the Old and the New World. One of the distinguishing features of this family is a long tail protruding beyond the wings. The European Free-tailed Bat prefers rocky countryside but also appears in towns. It leaves the roost before dusk and flies high, often in company with swifts. Although in the Mediterranean region it only lives in the warmest localities, it has been identified as far north as Switzerland. It also occurs in North Africa and in the Near East. We know little more about this species except that there is a single young, usually in June.

	Lhb (mm)	Lf (mm)	Wsp (mm)	W (g)
Barbastella barbastellus	44—59	35—42	254—268	6—10
Miniopterus schreibersi	48—63	42—48	280—305	8—17
Tadarida teniotis	82—87	58—64	410—450	20—50

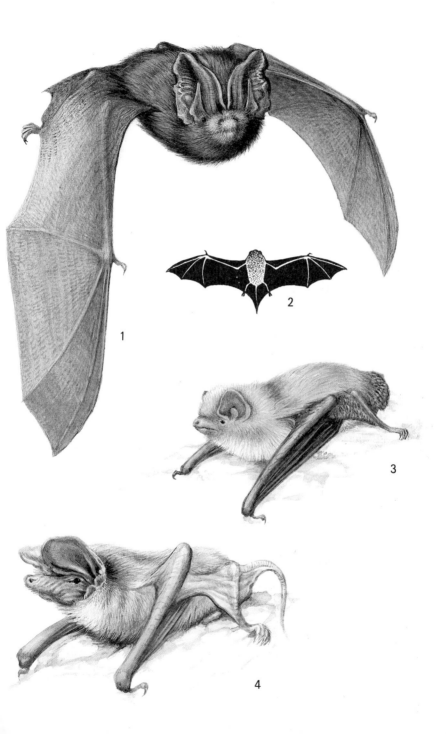

1

2

3

4

Barbary Ape
Macaca sylvanus

Order: Primates
Family: Cercopithecidae

The Barbary Ape (1) is regarded as the only monkey whose home range includes Europe, for it lives on the Rock of Gibraltar. It is not clear whether this was part of its natural range; it is far more likely to have been introduced at some time. In any case, the present population on Gibraltar has been augmented by animals caught in northwestern Africa. At present, there are about 40 Barbary Apes on Gibraltar. They live in two groups, one inhabiting the rocks of the fortress, the second the area between the rocks and the town. The monkeys are given food every day to prevent them coming into the town to forage. In North Africa, Barbary Apes are found in Algeria, in Morocco in the Jelaba Mountains, and at medium and higher elevations in the Atlas Mountains. They prefer rocky places overgrown with shrubs and thin woodland with streams or permanent water. Barbary Apes mostly live on the ground, climbing trees only to sleep or when in danger. They will also often spend the night under rock overhangs or in small caves.

Barbary Apes live in flocks of 12—30 members, each headed by an adult male. Group territories overlap and encounters of two groups result in minor skirmishes.

The sexual cycle of the female Barbary Ape lasts 27—30 days. In heat her sexual organs become swollen, being most noticeable between the 9th and the 11th day. The gestation period lasts approximately 8 $1/2$ months; a single young is usually born (2).

Like all primates, Barbary Apes are very communicative. Expressive gestures are as important as vocal signals. An impressive gesture is a menacing baring of the canines (3). Eyelid movement is also important. Barbary Apes may often be seen grubbing in each other's fur (4). This reciprocal grooming is of great social significance and is one of the factors determining rank in the hierarchy.

The Barbary Ape is now an endangered species in the wild. It used to occur in vast numbers over northwestern Africa, now it is found only in isolated areas. About 25,000 Barbary Apes now live in Algeria and Morocco but their numbers are decreasing rapidly. This is due to destruction of habitat, and to commercial hunting and capture. Several 'reserves' with breeding populations of Barbary Apes have been established in Germany and in France. The most famous are 'La Montagne des Singes' in the Vosges Mountains in France, the reserve at Salem near Lake Constance, and another near Rocamadur in southern France. These can now supply Barbary Apes to zoos and avoid the need to endanger the native wild population.

	L	H	W
Macaca sylvanus	60—75 cm	45—50 cm	5—15 (20) kg

Stoat or Ermine
Mustela erminea

Order: Carnivora
Family: Mustelidae

Although the Stoat is one of the most common predators, it is best known by its fur which was used to trim the cloaks of kings and caps of princes. Ermine is of course the winter fur, and in Britain is only produced in the north. The summer coat is brown (1), being replaced in winter (2) by the thick, pure white fur with a black tail tip that has been highly prized since ancient times. The Stoat is found all over Europe with the exception of the Mediterranean countries, and throughout northern Asia. It is widespread in the British Isles, being absent only from some islands, and has been introduced to the Shetland Islands. It is most often found in open, damp, shrubby habitats. A skilful climber and swimmer, it mainly eats rabbits, various rodents, birds and invertebrates, and occasionally takes fruit and other plant food. Mating takes place from July to September and from February to March. In females fertilized in winter the embryos develop normally with a gestation period of approximately 10 weeks, while in females fertilized in the autumn embryo development is delayed over the winter (latent pregnancy), and eight months elapse before the young are born. There are usually 3—9 young, tended by the male and the female.

The range of the Weasel (*M. nivalis*) includes practically all of Europe and Asia, as well as northwestern Africa. It is common in mainland Britain but is known only from the islands of Skye, Anglesey and the Isle of Wight, being absent from Ireland and most of the small islands. Populations living in the north or in high mountains (e.g. the Alps) turn white in winter but their tail lacks the black tip (4 shows their transient coat). However, in most of its range the Weasel keeps its brown coat summer and winter (3). Weasels vary considerably in size: the smallest subspecies may be found in the north, while in the south, especially around the Mediterranean where the Stoat is absent, the largest subspecies are found. Another characteristic is a marked sexual dimorphism, the females usually being much smaller than the males. Weasels live in similar habitats to Stoats but damp places are avoided. Their principal prey are mice and voles which are pursued even in their underground tunnels. Larger males sometimes hunt on the surface, preying on other mammals and birds. The main mating season usually falls in February and March, yet Weasels seem able to reproduce all the year round. Pregnancy lasts 33—35 days, and the number of young depends on the quantity of food available. When there is a population explosion amongst voles there may be as many as 12 weasel young in each litter; ordinarily, however, 3—7 young are usual.

Clawed toes are always visible in the prints of the Stoat's forepaw (5) and hindpaw (6), as well as in those of the Weasel's forepaw (7) and hindpaw (8).

The Siberian Weasel (*M. sibirica*) chiefly inhabits Asia. It lives in the Urals, reaching westward into Europe as far as Kirov, and is a typical forest-dweller which quite likes waterlogged sites. Rodents make up most of its diet. The mating season is in February and March. After 28—30 days of pregnancy the female bears 2—10 young, which are greyish-yellow in colour. The adult Siberian Weasel's fur is yellowish-orange and is relatively highly prized. It is sold as 'Kolin mink'.

	Lhb (mm)	Lt (mm)	W (g)
Mustela erminea	170—320	50—120	150—300
M. nivalis	110—260	12—87	30—160
M. sibirica	250—390	133—210	360—820

European Mink

Lutreola lutreola

Order: Carnivora
Family: Mustelidae

In the past the European Mink (1) was widespread in western, central and northern Europe where it mostly lived on the densely overgrown banks of rivers and lakes. In most of this area, however, it has been wiped out or greatly reduced in numbers, starting at the beginning of the present or towards the end of the last century. Although reduction in habitat as a result of man's cultivation may have contributed, it has even decreased in the relatively untouched forests of eastern Europe. Today the European Mink may be found for example in Finland, rarely in Poland and Rumania, and in very small numbers in western France.

The European Mink eats any animal it can find on the bank or in the water. Being an excellent diver, it can stay beneath the water for as long as two minutes. It excavates burrows in the bank, usually with two entrances. One of these is close to the level of the water, the second ends higher up the bank. The rutting season is usually in February, but may sometimes continue until April. After a gestation period of 35—42 days 2—7 young are born. At birth the young are ash-grey and start becoming darker at approximately one month old. Adult minks are predominantly dark brown to blackish-brown. It can easily be confused with the European Polecat in size, but polecats are never uniformly coloured and the white markings on the head are much more extensive than in mink.

The American Mink (*L. vison*) (2) is a native of the woodlands of North America. For more than a century, however, the mink has been ranch-reared for its fur. Today annual mink production world-wide represents about 24 million pelts. A number of fur farms were established in Europe, and American Mink escaping from these farms have given rise to feral populations. In the British Isles, feral mink have been reported from southern and northern England, south Wales, and southern Scotland. The American Mink was also deliberately introduced into some regions. Wherever the American Mink meets the European Mink, however, it is more successful than the latter and thus contributes to its extinction. The mating season sets in about four weeks earlier than that of the European Mink. Pregnancy lasts 36—75 days, the variability being due to an occasional brief latent period.

In the 1930s colour mutations started to appear in ranched American Mink. Some are very highly valued. Coloured mink are divided into groups. Recessive genes are involved in the blue (3), brown (4), beige and some white groups, and there is also a group with dominant colour mutations (5). Standard mink (those bearing the original colour) are grouped according to whether they are 'dark', 'extra dark', and 'extra extra dark', depending on the colour of the guard hair and whether the underfur has lost its brown hue.

	Lhb (mm)	Lt (mm)	W (g)	
Lutreola lutreola	280—430	120—190	550—800	
L. vison	300—600	158—194	600—800	in the wild
			800—2,500	in farms

European Polecat

Putorius putorius

Order: Carnivora
Family: Mustelidae

The European Polecat (1) is widespread throughout Europe with the exception of Ireland, northern Scandinavia, the Adriatic coast and the southern part of the Balkan Peninsula. To the east it reaches the Volga, the Don and the Urals. It is also found in northwestern Morocco. In Britain it is now extinct in Scotland and England but is found throughout Wales. Favourite habitats are fields, watersides, and forest margins, and it very often appears near farm buildings, sheltering in sheds, heaps of timber etc. It is predominantly nocturnal and feeds on everything from insects to smaller mammals, supplementing its diet from time to time with fruits and other plant food. Although it can climb and swim, it mostly hunts for food on the ground. The mating season lasts from February to May. After a pregnancy of 40—43 days the female gives birth to 3—8 young (called kittens). These are light-coloured at first, turning darker at 4—5 weeks, and may often be seen following their mother up to five months old. Prints of fore- (4) and hindpaws (5) are similar to those of martens but are proportionally smaller and are mostly found in mud near water. Their droppings are thin, often more than 5 cm long (6).

The Steppe or Asiatic Polecat (*Putorius eversmanni*) (2) inhabits southeastern Europe, reaching as far east as central Asia and northern India. It penetrates westwards to Austria, the Czech Republic and Germany and thrives in dry open areas, plains or cultivated plains. Its way of life is similar to that of the European Polecat but it often hides in underground burrows, mostly those deserted by sousliks and hamsters. Mating takes place in February and March, and gestation lasts 36—43 days. The Steppe Polecat usually produces more young than the European Polecat, sometimes more than 10 in a litter. Its diet is chiefly rodents, especially sousliks. The Steppe Polecat may be easily distinguished from the European Polecat by its colouring: the coat is lighter-coloured all over, especially in the middle of the body, with a contrasting dark tail tip. Facial markings are not particularly conspicuous.

The Marbled Polecat (*Vormela peregusna*) (3) is typically an inhabitant of Asia, from the Near East to Mongolia. Its European distribution is confined to the eastern part of the Balkan Peninsula and the Black Sea coast; in southern parts of former Yugoslavia it is a rare sight indeed. In the European part of its range it is becoming increasingly rare and tending to disappear. It lives on steppes, semi-deserts and deserts, hunting predominantly rodents. The mating season starts towards the end of winter and 4—8 young are born after a pregnancy of around 60 days. Very little is known about this species, but the male probably helps to look after the young.

All mustelids have well-developed scent glands on either side of the anus, which are used primarily for scent-marking. In the European, Steppe and Marbled Polecats, however, they are remarkably large and may also serve as a defence. The animal can empty them suddenly (when scared for example), scenting the neighbourhood so strongly that the enemy is deterred.

	Lhb (mm)	Lt (mm)	W (g)
Putorius putorius	310—480	110—210	500—2,000
P. eversmanni	320—560	80—180	480—2,000
Vormela peregusna	270—350	120—205	370—715

3

4

5

1

6

2

Beech or Stone Marten
Martes foina

Order: Carnivora
Family: Mustelidae

The range of the Beech Marten (1) includes the whole of Europe, excepting Britain, from the Baltic Sea southward as far as the Mediterranean islands, reaching across Asia Minor to central Asia. It is found in forest margins, in uneven terrain with plenty of hiding places, and on the Continent it even comes into large cities. It hunts by day and night but tends to become purely nocturnal wherever it is disturbed. It feeds on rodents — near human habitations Brown Rats (*Rattus norvegicus*) represent up to 80 per cent of its diet — and small birds, and plunders bird's nests. It is also very partial to fruit. The breeding season falls in July and August. Females that are not fertilized then come into heat again in February or March. The young are born from March to May. In females fertilized during the late summer there is a delay in implantation of the embryo, and a total pregnancy of eight months; females fertilized in spring progress through pregnancy without interruption and gestation takes no more than two months. The throat patch ('bib') is almost white, extending far down to the forelegs, with the exception of martens inhabiting Crete (*Martes foina cretica*) (4).

The Pine Marten (*M. martes*) (2) ranges from the Pyrenees throughout Europe as far north as the arctic treeline, in the Balkans as far as Macedonia, over the Near East eastward around to 80 °E. In the British Isles it is confined to the mountainous parts of Scotland, Wales, northern England and southern Ireland. The throat patch is yellowish to bright orange, and irregularly shaped. On the breast it narrows to a wedge and never reaches the forelegs. The Pine Marten is a typical inhabitant of woodland, hunting mainly at dusk or by night. It is an excellent climber, negotiating slender branches and leaping from tree to tree. The Pine Marten mainly eats rodents, and particularly seems to enjoy hunting squirrels. It often takes bats or birds that are resting in the trees, and also likes fruit. The mating period is in July and August, when the martens' loud squeals can often be heard. After a latent pregnancy throughout the winter the young are born in April or May. Until they are about 7 weeks they keep hidden in the nest which is usually in a hollow tree. After leaving the nest they continue to stay with their mother throughout the summer. Footprints (5) show the outline of five clawed toes. It is not easy to distinguish between the tracks of the two species. Droppings are less than 4 cm in length and taper slightly, often containing pips and seeds.

The Sable (*Martes zibellina*) (3) is an inhabitant of the Russian taiga and coniferous forests. Throughout history it has been hunted for its beautiful fur and disappeared from Scandinavia and Finland as early as the 10th century. Now Sables are extinct in Europe altogether. Their remaining range stretches throughout northern Asia as far as Japan, and here they are also on the wane. During the 20th century, numbers have been reduced by about 90 per cent. Where the Sable meets the Pine Marten, the two species interbreed giving rise to a range of hybrids. The Sable's diet consists mainly of rodents. It mates in July and August, but the implantation of the embryo is delayed until February—March. The young are born in March—May.

	Lhb (cm)	Lt (cm)	W (g)
Martes foina	38—60	23—32	950—2,100
M. martes	38—59	18—28	800—1,750
M. zibellina	32—46	14—28	900—1,800

Badger

Meles meles

Order: Carnivora
Family: Mustelidae

The Badger is found throughout Europe, with the exception of northern Scandinavia; it lives on Crete and in Asia Minor, from where its range extends to the Far East. In the British Isles it is widespread in England, Ireland and Wales, but is rarer in Scotland. Within its total range, there are three clearly distinct groups of subspecies differing both in colour and in size. Two of these groups inhabit the geographical region covered in this book. The boundary between them is the river Volga. To the west are the 'European' badgers (1, 2). These are larger, with a greyish-silvery colouring and a conspicuous mask, and live mainly in woods and forests. The range of the 'sand' badgers (3) stretches eastward. They are smaller, greyish-yellow, with a small mask, and live on the steppes.

Badgers spend most of the time underground. If they fail to find natural shelter amongst rocks, they dig sets, extensive systems of underground tunnels several dozen metres long and going down as deep as 3 metres below the surface. They do not normally emerge from these before dusk, yet in sheltered places they like to bask in the sun. They eat small animals but can be regarded as omnivores. They are far from choosey: besides various animals (insects, slugs, earthworms, small mammals, frogs and young birds) they also eat carrion, bird's eggs, and the fruits and roots of forest plants. Because they can eat a wide variety of food, their home range does not need to be very extensive; they never wander farther than 1—5 km from their sets. They use their acute sense of smell in their search for food, which is often accompanied by audible panting or grunting. In the autumn badgers put on a thick layer of fat under the skin. They hibernate from October until February but their winter sleep is often interrupted by brief periods of activity. This phenomenon is called false hibernation. In warm weather and in mild climates badgers do not hibernate at all. Their mating season lasts from July to September but varies from one part of the range to another: in some places it may set in at any time from January to October. In some females latent pregnancy (i.e. temporarily suspended development of the embryo) has been observed, in others the development of the embryo proceeds without interruption. Gestation periods thus vary widely, between 7 and 15 months. Each litter comprises 1—5 young which are suckled by the female for 2—3 months. Newborn cubs are blind and covered with sparse white hairs. Their eyes open and teeth come through after 30 days or so. Towards the end of summer the cubs begin to fend for themselves but very often remain with their mother (4) throughout the winter. Badgers do not live in seclusion, one set often harbours several families, and individual families often 'visit' each other. Pairs usually remain faithful throughout life. Usually it is only the front part of the sole, the five long toes and strong claws, that shows in a badger's track. When the entire underside of the foot is impressed, the track may be as much as 11 cm long (5, forepaw; 6, hindpaw). The prints of all toes point inwards, hind tracks almost always partially overlap the fore tracks. The badger's droppings (7) are bluntly pointed at one end and contain the wing cases of beetles, and also pips and fruit skins.

	Lhb	Lt	W
Meles meles	60—90 cm	11—24 cm	7—24 kg

1

2

3

4

5

7

6

Wolverine or Glutton
Gulo gulo

Order: Carnivora
Family: Mustelidae

Today the Wolverine (1, 2) is sparsely distributed in Norway, Sweden and northern Finland, and across the entire taiga and tundra zone of Europe, Asia and North America. However, as late as the 1930s Wolverines lived all along the Gulf of Finland, and earlier in parts of European Russia and Poland. Wolverine numbers are now small and territories occupied by individual animals are very extensive — from 200 to 1,600 km². The size of the hunting area depends on several factors — terrain, prevailing food supplies, and climate. Territories of males are two to three times larger than those of females. Wolverines mark the boundaries of their territories with secretions from their anal scent glands (3). Although they are mostly nocturnal, in regions with a long polar night they prefer to hunt in the light part of the day. In spring the Wolverine mostly feeds on the eggs of ground-nesting birds as well as on the birds themselves. When forest fruits begin to ripen it takes raspberries, blueberries and cranberries. It also roots for wasp nests to feast on their larvae and pupae, and hunts Mountain Hares. In winter, in snow, even large animals fall prey to the Wolverine. It hunts Roe Deer, Red Deer and Elk, and is said to pursue Foxes, and even Wolves, driving other predators from their prey which it then takes. Carrion constitutes a relatively large part of its diet, and it is often preferred to hunting live prey. Wolverines have very powerful teeth and a massive skull with an outstanding sagittal ridge (4). The Wolverine does not make a permanent home for the winter. It can often be found under the snow-covered, sweeping branches of spruces and firs, and sometimes digs small snow caves. The young are reared in relatively deep burrows, up to 20 m long, in the ground or in the snow, lined with moss and dry grass. Wolverines mate from April to June but it is probable that, in some areas, females may be fertilized at other times. Pregnancy is usually prolonged by a latent period, the 'real' pregnancy taking around 2 months. The young are born in February and March. Most often there are 2—3 to a litter; they stay with their mother until the following spring. The newborn young are relatively underdeveloped, weighing only 300—600 g. Their eyes do not open until 5 weeks old. At 3 months they are weaned. Up to the age of 7—8 weeks they are covered with a light, greyish-yellow fur, which is then replaced by the uniformly dark brown coat borne by young Wolverines up to one year old when they exchange it for the adult coat.

There are many myths connected with the Wolverine which are essentially similar in Lapp, Eskimo, Red Indian and Mongolian folklore. The Wolverine is considered to be an incarnation of the devil, a malefactor metamorphosed into an animal, a 'Wild Hunter'. It is advisable not to mention it at all. However, even modern hunters will agree that the Wolverine is a mysterious animal which is rarely encountered and usually escapes from every trap.

	Lhb	Lt	W
Gulo gulo	70—105 cm	13—23 cm	15—45 kg

Otter
Lutra lutra

Order: Carnivora
Family: Mustelidae

The Otter (1, 2) ranges across the whole of Europe and Asia, with the exception of the far north. In north Africa it is found in Algeria and Morocco. The Otter is now rarely seen in the British Isles. It is most common in Ireland and in southwest England, while elsewhere in England few probably remain. It is semi-aquatic and likes unpolluted waters, running or still, with rough banks providing plenty of shelter. In the west of Scotland, Otters live by the sea, feeding on sea fish. They excavate burrows (holts) in the banks which open under the water. There is usually a main holt and several shallow secondary burrows. The Otter is an excellent swimmer (3) capable of making long dives, remaining submerged for as long as 4 minutes. Its cylindrical body offers little resistance to the water, the tail is used as a rudder, the short and powerful legs with webbed toes serve as paddles. When the Otter is underwater, its nose and ears are closed off by hairs. Long tactile whiskers on the snout enable the Otter to navigate in muddy water and when crawling through burrows. The Otter is essentially a fish-eater, but also catches crayfish, rodents, birds, frogs and insects. It usually hunts by night and eats its prey on the bank or on stones jutting out into the water (4). Sometimes the remains of a meal can be found in such places. The Otter's presence is also betrayed by tracks (5, forepaw; 6, hindpaw) and droppings deposited in conspicuous places as an olfactory and visual signal (7). The Otter is a relatively large animal consuming around a kilogram of food per day on average. Consequently its hunting grounds are fairly extensive, sometimes up to about 30 km of running water. This is one of the reasons that Otters are relatively rare and never occur in great numbers.

Otters associate for mating in the first 6 months of the year. The rutting season is usually from February to June, but mating can evidently occur at any time of the year judging from the appearance of cubs in any month. Gestation takes about 63 days but sometimes pregnancy may last 9—10 months due to delayed implantation. There are usually 2—4 cubs in a litter. At about 31—34 days their eyes open. They are taken to the water at the age of 10 weeks and stay with their mother for almost a year. At first the male helps in tending the young. Sexual maturity is attained at 2—3 years. When they set out to look for a hunting ground of their own, they travel long distances and may often be found well away from water.

Otters have been hunted for their thick fur since ancient times and this ultimately led to their disappearance from many areas. In the recent past, however, the pollution and damming of running waters have contributed to their extinction, particularly in Europe. The Otter is now included in the list of species threatened with extinction and most countries take measures for its protection. It is hopeful that wherever rivers have become free of pollution, Otters are again increasing in numbers. The future of the Otter in Europe lies entirely in man's hands.

Young Otters living in the wild like to play and make slides down steep banks. When cared for by humans, they readily become domesticated.

	Lhb	Lt	W
Lutra lutra	57—90 cm	30—55 cm	4—16 kg

1

2

3

4

5

6

7

Brown Bear
Ursus arctos

Order: Carnivora
Family: Ursidae

In the remote past the Brown Bear (1) inhabited almost all Europe, northern Asia and North America. It was still common in Britain at the time of the Romans, surviving in Scotland perhaps until the 9th century. Large beasts of prey, however, cannot survive the spread of civilization and land cultivation. Today bears survive only where they can avoid man—in the mountains, in extensive forests, and in remote regions. There are now very few bears left in Europe. The largest numbers are thought to be in Rumania and countries of former Yugoslavia. Isolated records have also been reported from Bulgaria, the Czech Republic, Finland, France, Greece, Italy, Norway, Poland, Sweden and Spain. In the countries of the former USSR bears are still relatively common. In areas where they are not persecuted or disturbed, bears are active in daytime but for the most part man has compelled them to turn to an exclusively nocturnal way of life. Bears live alone except in the mating season and when they tend the young, several individuals often being found together at these times. The bear spends the winter in false hibernation from which it often awakes to leave its den in search of food. The bear is an omnivore; besides animals of all kinds including carrion, it eats fruits and seeds, and visits fields to take maize cobs, for example. The mating season starts in April and ends in July. The actual development of the embryo does not take more than 8 to 10 weeks but due to a latent period pregnancy lasts 7–9 months. The female gives birth to her young, usually two in a litter, during the dormant winter period. The cubs are very immature when born, approximately 20 cm long and 500 g in weight. At about 4 weeks they open their eyes, and do not leave the den for 3 months. They are suckled for about 4 months (2) and stay with their mother for 2–3 years. Older bear cubs are exceedingly lively and very good at climbing (3). Young bears attain sexual maturity from 4 years of age.

Syria, Asia Minor, Iran and the Caucasus are the home of a distinctly different race of bear, the Syrian Bear (*Ursus arctos syriacus*) (4). It is smaller than European bears, yellowish-brown in colour, and even the claws on its feet are light-coloured. This bear is seriously endangered. It is included in the 'Red Data Book' of the International Union for the Conservation of Nature (IUCN) as threatened with impending extinction. From fossils found in northwestern Africa, in Morocco, this bear probably existed there in historical times.

The home range of an individual bear is extensive, covering up to several thousand hectares. The bear continuously roams its territory, marking it with piles of droppings, peeling strips of bark off certain trees up to a height of 2 m and rubbing its back against the wood. It leaves behind traces of its claws and scent markings. The skull is massive, with undifferentiated carnassials and powerful ridges at the back of the brain case (5). The imprint of the forepaw (7) usually shows no more than the clawed toes and a small part of the sole, while the hindpaw is impressed in its entirety (6).

	Lhb	Lt	W
Ursus arctos	150—200 cm	6—14 cm	120—400 kg

Polar Bear
Thalarctos maritimus

Order: Carnivora
Family: Ursidae

The home of the Polar Bear (1, 5, skull) is the northern polar region. Some live on ice floes which may carry them as far as the North Pole, others permanently inhabit coastal areas. Polar Bears cross the sea from Spitzbergen to the Norwegian coast, and from Greenland to Iceland. They are strong swimmers and may be encountered far off in the open ocean. Polar Bears are vagrant, travelling long distances both actively and passively on drifting ice floes. Only females lead a settled life when they rear the young. Their home is the sea and so, when on land, they never venture more than a few kilometres away from the water. The Polar Bear's diet consists predominantly of aquatic mammals and fish, and in summer birds and their eggs as well. Terrestrial mammals are seldom hunted. Seals and walruses form almost 70 per cent of their food, fish represent a little less than 30 per cent, and the rest consists of other animals and, rarely, plants — marine algae and mosses. The hard conditions of the Arctic often make hunting impossible and Polar Bears starve for long periods. Whenever food is available, however, they can eat extraordinary quantities. The stomach of one bear killed in Franz Josef Land contained 41 kg of meat and fish! This was an exception as in normal circumstances Polar Bears eat 6—8 kg of meat at a meal.

The onset of the breeding season is toward the end of spring or at the beginning of summer, varying with the area. After a pregnancy of about eight months (230—250 days), the female gives birth to her cubs in a den excavated in the snow or ice (2). The den is usually 160—180 cm high and may be up to 260 cm long when the female has a greater number of cubs. An air-shaft leads to the outside. Females pregnant for the first time bear a single cub, older females produce 2, rarely 3 or even 4 young. The newborn cubs are blind, almost naked, weighing around 500 g. Their eyes only open after a month. Milk teeth (incisors and canines) start coming through at $1^{1}/_{2}$—2 months. When transferred by their mother from one place to another, the cubs do not roll themselves up in a ball as do other beasts of prey but hang rigid and motionless (3). They stay with their mother for two seasons (4) and reach sexual maturity at 3—4 years. The female bears young only every other year, and the reproductive capacity of Polar Bears is therefore low. When she has lost her young for some reason, she comes into heat again and may produce a second litter of cubs. Polar Bears have been hunted for years by the Eskimo, but this in itself did not endanger the existence of the species. In the 17th and 18th centuries however, hunters, whalers and fur traders started to come into the Arctic, and this marked the onset of intensive hunting. In the 1830s over 2,000 Polar Bears were being killed each year. It was only in 1965 that measures were taken to protect them and today commercial hunting is forbidden.

	Lhb	Lt	W
Thalarctos maritimus	160—250 cm	8—10 cm	400—450 kg

European, Feline or Small-spotted Genet
Genetta genetta

Order: Carnivora
Family: Viverridae

Genets are small, spotted beasts of prey only rarely encountered in the wild. They are exclusively nocturnal and also very retiring. Their European distribution includes Spain, southern France and the Balearic Islands; rare records have also been reported from southern Germany, Switzerland and Belgium. Around the Mediterranean they live in north Africa, and in the Near East and Middle East. The European Genet (1) extends southwards across the whole of Africa, excluding the Sahara. Its favourite habitats are woods and dry grasslands. It hides in dense vegetation, in rocks, and in deserted buildings. Being an adept climber, it is also found in hollow trees. The European Genet takes small rodents, birds, reptiles and insects, and less commonly various fruit.

European Genets are solitary. Pairs come together in the mating season, usually in spring and towards the end of summer, when they can sometimes be detected by a mewing sound. Pregnancy lasts 70—80 days, with 2—5 young in a litter. Most females bear young only once, exceptionally twice, a year. The young are born blind and covered with a short downy hair which quite clearly shows the typical spotted pattern. At about three weeks the young leave the nest to roam about with their mother for some time to come.

Another representative of the civet-cat family is the Ichneumon or Egyptian Mongoose (*Herpestes ichneumon*) (2). It lives in the southeast of the Iberian Peninsula, in north Africa and the Near East, extending southward across Africa excepting the rainforest. It has been introduced onto the island of Mijet in the Adriatic. It prefers dense vegetation and likes to stay near water. Invertebrate animals and various fruit form the greater part of its diet, but it also hunts various small vertebrates including fish. Ichneumons are diurnal and are sometimes active on a clear moonlit night. They prefer living alone, only occasionally occurring in pairs. Heaps of stones, rocky places and the deserted burrows of other animals provide shelter, but they excavate their own burrows on rare occasions. It seems that mating is not confined to any particular time of the year. Gestation lasts 55—65 days, and a litter usually contains 2—4 young. The female dislikes disturbance of any kind and at the slightest suspicion will move the whole litter to another place.

In comparison with the skull of the European Genet (4), the Ichneumon's skull (5) has closed eyeholes, a longish-oval brain case, and a relatively wide space between the eyes.

The Indian Mongoose (*Herpestes edwardsii*) (3), was introduced to southern Italy around 1960. This species is widespread in southwestern Asia, extending over Afghanistan and Iran as far as Iraq. It is famous for hunting venomous snakes, such as the cobra. Although it is not immune against snake venom it can tolerate a dose about six times stronger than, for example, a rabbit. Its general biology is similar to that of the Ichneumon.

	Lhb (cm)	Lt (cm)	W (kg)
Genetta genetta	40—55	40—50	1.3—2.35
Herpestes ichneumon	45—60	35—60	1.9—4.0
H. edwardsii	35—45	35—40	1.2—1.5

Striped or Laughing Hyena

Order: Carnivora

Hyaena hyaena

Family: Hyaenidae

The Striped Hyena (1) is widespread in the dry grasslands, semi-deserts and deserts of north Africa, through Arabia to the Near East and Asia Minor. In the east it is found in the Indian Peninsula, reaching northwards into southern central Asia. In Africa it lives in the Sudanese part of the Sahel, and east Africa down to Tanzania. It is nocturnal, hiding during the day in burrows, caves and dense scrub. Hyenas are mostly carrion-eaters, crushing even large bones with their powerful teeth (2) to extract the marrow. Occasionally they also hunt live prey, mainly young ungulates. Fruit is also a part of their diet, and they come into gardens and oases to look for it. The Striped Hyena is a quiet creature whose long-drawn-out howls are rarely heard. The mating season falls in January and February but is repeated several times a year. After a pregnancy of approximately 90 days, 2—4 young are born blind and covered with greyish white fur bearing the characteristic stripes. The eyes open after about a week. The young are suckled for two months, and then are fed on flesh brought by both parents. The whole family stays together for a long time and shares a sleeping chamber in a common lair.

The hyena is often confused with the African Hunting Dog or Painted Hyena (*Lycaon pictus*) (3), even though its different stature and markings are easily recognizable. This belongs to the dog family (Canidae). The African Hunting Dog is still common in sub-Saharan Africa and is occasionally seen in southern Algeria.

African Hunting Dogs hunt in the daytime in packs which are formed most frequently by members of a single family. The hunting range of an individual pack is very extensive. They are extremely agile and voracious predators eating their prey on the spot immediately after bringing the animal down, often while it is still alive. They chiefly hunt small ungulates. The pack is a social unit and all adults share in the care of the young. Breeding takes place all year round. After a pregnancy of 69—72 days the female usually gives birth to 2—6 young, but litters of 12—18 have also been reported.

In the Sahara lives one of the smallest members of the dog family, the Fennec (*Fennecus zerda*) (4). The Fennec is nocturnal, preying on small rodents, reptiles and insects. During the day it hides in burrows. Though it lives in groups, each animal hunts by itself. Fennecs mate in early spring and the young (usually two) are born in March and April after a pregnancy of 50 days. The Sand Fox (*Vulpes rüppelli*) (5) is a little larger than the Fennec and also lives in the Sahara. The biology of both species is similar. The Sand Fox is easily identified by its white tail tip.

	Lhb (cm)	Lt (cm)	W (kg)
Hyaena hyaena	110—120	30—35	30—40
Lycaon pictus	100—110	35—40	25—37
Fennecus zerda	30—40	20—24	1.5—2.3
Vulpes rüppelli	40—50	25—30	2.5—3

Wolf

Canis lupus

Order: Carnivora
Family: Canidae

In the past the Wolf (1) was common throughout Europe but has been driven out by advancing cultivation and forest clearance, disappearing from most of western Europe in historical times. The last wolves lived in England and Wales in the 16th century. It became extinct in Scotland in the late 17th century and in Ireland towards the end of the 18th century. Wolves are now found only on the Iberian Peninsula, in Italy and on Sicily in western Europe. The present continuous distribution of the Wolf extends eastwards from a line running through northern Scandinavia, the Baltic States, Poland, the Carpathians and the Balkan Peninsula. It is found throughout Asia and in North America from Alaska to Mexico. Wolves inhabit most types of environment, from dense forests to steppes and semi-deserts, from the subtropics to the polar regions. Within this vast range several subspecies have arisen which differ in size and colour. (The dimensions given below apply to European wolves.)

Wolves live in family groups composed of a parental pair together with their current young and the sexually immature young born the year before. In winter, several groups sometimes unite to form larger packs, which communicate by howling (2). In summer wolves take chiefly small mammals, birds, and some plant food, while in winter they hunt large ungulates, mainly deer. Hunting grounds covered by a pack are extensive, up to 50 km². Wolves mate early in the year when the pack temporarily breaks up. The female digs a burrow where 1—14 blind cubs (3) are born after 62—75 days pregnancy. The male helps to feed and rear the young which attain sexual maturity at around 2—3 years old.

The home of the Golden or Indian Jackal (*Canis aureus*) (4) is southeastern Europe as far north as Hungary and Slovenia, then the Near East and the whole of southern Asia, as well as north and east Africa. It likes habitats with plenty of shelter — thickets, rocks and reed-beds for example — and avoids open steppes. The Golden Jackal is predominantly nocturnal and lives in pairs. It hunts smaller mammals and birds, and also scavenges for carrion and garbage around towns, villages and farms. Fruit and other plant food also form part of its diet. In the evening the jackals' long-drawn-out howling can be heard, interrupted by barking. The mating period is in January and February. Pregnancy lasts 58—65 days and 3—8 young are born in a burrow excavated by both parents. The young are suckled for 6—8 weeks but at three weeks their parents begin to give them predigested and disgorged meat. The young start hunting on their own at the early age of 2 months and leave the parents in the autumn. Jackals soon attain sexual maturity, males commonly at 10 months, females around 1¹/₂ years, but often earlier.

Our domesticated dogs are descended from the Wolf, and in the opinion of some, the Golden Jackal also has a part in their ancestry, at least in some regions of Africa. Domestication is thought to have started around 6,000—10,000 years ago.

Both the Wolf (5) and the Golden Jackal (6) have a characteristically elongated skull with a long jaw. The brain case of the Wolf's skull bears a marked sagittal ridge.

	Lhb (cm)	Lt (cm)	W (kg)
Canis lupus	105—160	35—60	30—60
C. aureus	71—85	20—30	7—15

Red Fox
Vulpes vulpes

Order: Carnivora
Family: Canidae

The Red Fox (1) is found all over Europe (except for Iceland), most of Asia, North Africa and North America. It is common on the British mainland, but is absent from the Orkneys and Shetlands, and also from the Scottish islands with the exception of Skye. It inhabits all types of environment from the lowlands up to the mountains, forests, grassland, cultivated land and even towns. Thanks to its covert way of life, it successfully escapes notice even in parks and wasteland in large cities. It is a remarkably variable species, especially in colour. Colour and size vary both within individual populations and in different geographical regions, for example foxes from the Ukrainian steppes are smaller and lighter-coloured than those from the European woodlands. Populations of Red Foxes quite often include individuals who seem to have lost colour, and are of a yellowish hue, or individuals with a dark band along the back and across the shoulder-blades (2), or with dark-coloured underparts. Foxes with a black ground colour (so-called silver foxes) (3) are sometimes found in America and in some parts of Siberia. If such a fox is found in Europe it is sure to have escaped from a fur-farm. Foxes are solitary and active mostly by night, particularly where they are hunted. Their diet consists largely of small rodents and invertebrates, and they will also take rabbits and birds. They supplement the diet by the fruits of forest shrubs. Foxes mate in January and February, copulation usually taking place in the 'earth' (den). After a gestation period of 51—53 days, the vixen gives birth to 3—6, rarely as many as 10, cubs. They are suckled for 6 weeks but at 4 weeks the mother starts to give them disgorged flesh. Cubs begin to fend for themselves at about 3 months old. Fox tracks (as in all canine species) are four-toed with clearly defined claw marks (6, forefoot; 7, hindfoot).

The polar regions and the northernmost parts of Europe, Asia and America are the home of the Arctic Fox (*Alopex lagopus*). This has a summer and a winter coat. The summer fur is short, whereas the winter fur is long and thick, in some individuals changing to a greyish-blue (4), in others to pure white (5). Arctic Foxes also change their habitat with the seasons. In spring and summer, when they mate and reproduce, they live on the tundra. In winter they move north, to the ice fields of the Arctic Ocean, and floating ice floes can take them as far as the North Pole. But some Arctic Foxes move southwards for the winter along river valleys or mountain ranges, coming relatively far into the forest belt. The Arctic Fox feeds mainly on rodents, especially lemmings, on birds and their eggs, and in winter on anything that is cast up by the sea. The vixen is pregnant for 49—56 days and gives birth to 3—12 cubs, the number in a litter largely depending on the food supply available and on the mother's condition. The winter fur of the Arctic Fox is highly valued and now mostly comes from farm-bred animals.

	Lhb (cm)	Lt (cm)	W (kg)
Vulpes vulpes	50—80	30—50	3—10
Alopex lagopus	45—75	25—30	2—6

Raccoon Dog
Nyctereutes procyonoides

Order: Carnivora
Family: Canidae

The Raccoon Dog (1) is an Asiatic beast of prey native to the Far East and Japan, where it lives in damp places, forests and reed-beds. It is omnivorous, and hunts at night. It is hunted for its fur and was introduced in the 1930s to various European parts of the former USSR from where it has spread westwards. Today it can be found in many European countries, in Finland and Sweden to the north, the Netherlands to the west, and as far south as Switzerland.

It is the only member of the dog family that spends the winter in hibernation, in this case false hibernation, lasting from December until April. On warm days, Raccoon Dogs leave their dens and then their tracks (2, forefoot; 3, hindfoot) can be sometimes found in snow. Mating takes place from February to April. After a gestation period of 58—65 days the female gives birth to 3—15 young, which are also tended by the male. The whole family stays together until the end of August. The young mature very rapidly, at 8—10 months.

Another alien brought to Europe as a result of the fur-trade is the Raccoon (*Procyon lotor*) (4), a member of the Procyonidae (raccoons and allies). Its original home is North and Central America, where it thrives in woodlands and scrub, usually near water. It is extremely adaptable, and today is also found in open country. Raccoons live singly and hunt at night. They are agile climbers and good swimmers and take a varied diet. From its behaviour in captivity a mistaken assumption that the raccoon 'washes' its food has been made. However, this habit has given it its popular name in several European languages (*Waschbär, raton laveur*). In the wild, raccoons search for their food on land and in water, where they feel for it with their forepaws (5), whereas in captivity they find all their food on the ground. However, the inborn behaviour pattern governing their search for food asserts itself and they take some food into water and 'search' for it there — hence the 'washing'. At present, several feral Raccoon populations are known in Europe, formed both by escapees from fur-farms, and by animals intentionally introduced into some parts of Germany and the former USSR. Permanent feral populations exist at present in Hessen, Rhineland-Westphalia and Thuringia, Germany, in the Netherlands and in the western part of the former USSR.

Raccoons breed in January and February. Each male mates with several females who subsequently found their own independent families. The young are born in litters of 3—4 from April to June, after a pregnancy of 60—70 days. The newborn young are fully furred and bear the typical masklike facial markings, but they are blind. Their eyes open at about 18 days. At 10 weeks they leave the nest.

On the lower jaw of the Raccoon Dog there is a conspicuous notch below the inconspicuous angular process (6). The Raccoon's skull has a relatively short facial part and in some ways resembles that of a mustelid (weasel family) (7). The canines are almost undifferentiated from the other teeth, an indication of its omnivorous diet.

	Lhb (cm)	Lt (cm)	W (kg)
Nyctereutes procyonoides	65—80	15—25	4—12
Procyon lotor	50—60	20—30	3.5—10

European Wild Cat
Felis silvestris

Order: Carnivora
Family: Felidae

The European Wild Cat (1) was once a common representative of the felids in Europe. But hand in hand with the disappearance of its preferred forest habitats and their transformation into cultivated land, its numbers have been decreasing and it has disappeared altogether from many areas. Where it has survived, mostly in the warm, deciduous forests of hilly areas, it lives in concealment and easily escapes notice. Permanent populations still exist in Scotland (elsewhere in Britain it became extinct in the 1850s), in Portugal, Spain, France, Belgium and Germany. It is still relatively common in some parts of southern Europe and in eastern central Europe. The eastern distribution of the European Wild Cat ends in the Caucasus and in woodlands alongside the lower course of the Dnieper and Dniester rivers, while in the southeast it extends to Asia Minor.

Cats living in north Africa (and throughout Africa) and in the Near East have shorter fur, less conspicuous body markings and no dark band on their backs. These are African Wild Cats (*Felis lybica*) (2). Further to the east, into central Asia and westwards to the Astrakhan district lies the home of the Steppe Cat (*Felis ornata*) (7), whose fur is spotted instead of striped. The biology of all these species is similar, the only difference being that the Steppe Cat and the African Wild Cat typically inhabit open country. All three live chiefly on rodents, only exceptionally capturing larger mammals such as hares. They breed at the beginning of the year, with a gestation period of 63—68 days. In a nest in a rock cleft, or a hollow tree or in an abandoned fox's earth or badger's set, the female gives birth to 2—4, rarely up to 6, kittens. Their eyes open at 9—11 days. The female suckles her young for about 6 weeks. Female kittens are mature at 10 months, males not usually before 3 years.

All these three species are probably ancestors of the domestic cat (*Felis cattus*). The African Wild Cat probably made the greatest contribution as, in contrast to the other two, it does not shun man and may often be found near human settlements. It is often difficult to distinguish between the European Wild Cat and a 'wild-coloured' domestic cat. The most reliable identifying features are the shape of the tail (4) which is much thicker and blunt-ended (cf. the slender pointed tail of the domestic cat, 5) and the undersurface of the hindpaws which are dark only at the end, whereas in the domestic cat they are dark all over.

The deserts and savannas in north Africa, Arabia, southwestern Asia and the Transcaspian region are the home of the rare Sand Cat (*Felis margarita*) (3). It feeds almost exclusively on small rodents which it hunts by night. Little is known about its biology. Mating takes place at the beginning of the year, and the female gives birth to 2—4 young at the beginning of April. Kittens are of course born blind and, unlike other cat species, their eyes open relatively late, not before the 16th day. Kittens also start taking solid food later than other cats. Sandy deserts offer the Sand Cat little natural shelter and it often excavates shallow burrows, unlike the other wild cats.

The felid skull is rounded, with a shortened face, powerful jaws, and a small sagittal ridge (6).

	Lhb (cm)	Lt (cm)	W (kg)
Felis silvestris	45—60	23—35	2—13
F. lybica	43—60	23—40	1.5—6
F. ornata	55—75	23—33	2.5—8
F. margarita	46—57	29—34	1.5—3

1

2

3

4

5

6

7

Lynx or **Northern Lynx**

Lynx lynx

Order: Carnivora
Family: Felidae

Long ago the Lynx (1) lived in the forests throughout Europe, northern Asia and North America. Today, however, it can only be found in Scandinavia, in the Carpathians and in the Balkan Mountains; from Poland it stretches eastward across the northern part of the former USSR, and also occurs in North America. In 1970 the Northern Lynx was reintroduced to former Yugoslavia, Switzerland and Austria. It leads a solitary life in forests with dense undergrowth or in rocky areas. The main prey are ungulates, mostly Roe Deer and Red Deer, but also Wild Boar. In summer it also hunts hares, rodents, birds, and takes invertebrates. It pursues its prey either by stalking or jumping out from ambush or down from a rock or other high place. Mating takes place in February and March. After a gestation period of 70–75 days 2–4 kittens are born in a sheltered spot, usually under an uprooted tree or between rocks. Their eyes open at about 16 days, and the female suckles for about three months. The young stay with their mother until the next mating season when the family breaks up. The young take 2–3 years to attain sexual maturity. Lynx tracks are distinctly rounded and do not show claws (4, forefoot; 5 hindfoot).

The Iberian Peninsula is the home of the Pardel or Spanish Lynx (*Lynx pardina*) (2). Numbers started to diminish at the beginning of the present century and an alarming reduction was recorded in the 1950s and 1960s when it was wiped out from a great many areas. It is an inhabitant of open coppices and forests with sparse undergrowth and depends mainly on rabbits for its food. The epidemic of myxomatosis which decimated the rabbit populations in the 1950s and 1960s was therefore also a tragedy for the Pardel. Its reproductive behaviour is similar to that of the Northern Lynx.

The Leopard or Panther (*Panthera pardus*) (3) is a well-known predator from tropical Africa and Asia, but is less generally known to live also in north Africa, the Near East, and even Turkey. There are around 100 individuals in the Atlas Mountains, small numbers in Syria and Israel, and in Turkey, particularly in western Anatolia, there are at present about 20 Leopards. Once Leopards were common in the Caucasus but are now extinct there. Leopards inhabit all types of country but prefer scrubby, rocky terrain offering plenty of shelter. Their diet consists largely of ungulates. If these are not plentiful they will also hunt small mammals and birds, and occasionally reptiles. Mating is not restricted to a particular part of the year but most frequently takes place from February to June. Pregnancy lasts for 90—105 days and there are 1—4, rarely up to 6, kittens. After having left the nest the young stay with their mother for quite a long time, sometimes for more than a year. The Leopard is now threatened with extinction, and, with the exception of Nigeria, South Africa and Namibia, it is protected everywhere by law.

	Lhb (cm)	Lt (cm)	W (kg)
Lynx lynx	80—130	15—25	15—36
L. pardina	80—110	12—14	14—25
Panthera pardus	100—160	75—110	30—80

Common or Harbour Seal
Phoca vitulina

Order: Pinnipedia
Family: Phocidae

The Common Seal (1) lives in coastal waters on both sides of the Atlantic and the Pacific Oceans. In Europe it is found from Finland to Portugal, being most common along the North Sea coasts and in the Baltic, as far north as Stockholm, but is absent from the Gulf of Finland and the Gulf of Bothnia. Along the eastern coast of England, on the Shetlands, Orkneys and Hebrides, the western coast of Scotland and the eastern coast of Ireland it often appears in remarkable numbers, especially during the breeding season. It favours shallow water close to sandy shores, and quite often wanders inland along large rivers. In the breeding season colonies assemble chiefly on the Shetlands, the Orkneys, along the northern coast of England and in the southwest. They also appear on the northeastern coast of Ireland. The Common Seal lives chiefly on fish, with crustacea and molluscs forming a small part of the diet. The favourite food of newly weaned pups, however, are shrimps. The Common Seal often lives in shallow waters and on suitable shores in groups of several hundred. Pups are born from May to June, weighing around 12 kg when newborn. They are always suckled on land. Mating takes place soon after the young have been born. The gestation period lasts 11 months.

The Ringed Seal (*Pusa hispida*) (2) is the most common seal of the Arctic regions. It is also found in Iceland and in the Gulf of Bothnia, the Gulf of Finland, and in some lakes in the former USSR and Finland. Stragglers occasionally appear off the coast of Germany, the Netherlands, Ireland and England. Ringed Seals in the Arctic give birth to their young on drifting ice floes or on the ice fields surrounding the North Pole. Like all other seals the female produces a single pup, which is born in March or April and weighs about 5 kg. Before delivery the female digs a den in the snow or finds a small natural ice cave. The actual gestation period of eight months is prolonged by a latent period (the egg does not start developing immediately after fertilization, its implantation in the uterus being delayed by $3^1/_2$ months) to $11—11^1/_2$ months. Unlike the Common Seal, the Ringed Seal takes mainly crustacea; it also hunts small fish up to about 15 cm in size.

Two other seals inhabiting the Arctic Atlantic are also found on the northern coasts of Sweden and Finland and in the White Sea. These are the Harp Seal (*Pagophilus groenlandicus*) (3) and the Bearded Seal (*Erignathus barbatus*) (4). Individuals occasionally wander as far as the North Sea and the British coast. From time to time the Harp Seal makes an appearance off the Shetlands, off the Scottish coast and further to the south as far as Devon. The Bearded Seal sometimes visits the coasts of Scotland and Norfolk. The Harp Seal is a typical inhabitant of the open sea and floating ice floes, the Bearded Seal prefers to stay close to the coast. In both these species gestation is interrupted by delayed implantation of the egg.

Seals moving on snow leave a characteristic track (5).

	L (cm)	W (kg)
Phoca vitulina	160—200	50—150
Pusa hispida	130—150	35—125
Pagophilus groenlandicus	150—220	140—160
Erignathus barbatus	190—250	225—350

1

2

4

5

3

♂

♀

Grey or Atlantic Seal
Halichoerus gryphus

Order: Pinnipedia
Family: Phocidae

Exposed rocky coasts on both sides of the northern Atlantic are the home of the Grey Seal (1, 2). In Europe it is found as far south as northern Spain and Portugal. It also occurs in the Baltic Sea and in the Gulf of Bothnia. Around 65 per cent of the total world population live in the coastal waters around the British Isles. The largest breeding colonies have been reported from the Orkney Islands and the Scottish coast. Atlantic populations usually give birth to their young between September and December, Baltic populations in spring. Pregnancy lasts around $11^1/_2$ months, with a latent period of around three months. The main item in the Grey Seal's diet is fish, particularly those of open waters. It also eats crustacea and molluscs from the sea floor. When hunting it may dive to a depth of more than 100 m.

The Monk Seal (*Monachus monachus*) (3) used to be very common in the Mediterranean and in the Black Sea. Today, however, it has become relatively rare and has disappeared altogether from many areas. Traditional breeding beaches are now crowded with tourists. Nowadays it is most common on Corsica, in the Gulf of Salonika, on Rhodes and on the Turkish coast. Outside the Mediterranean the Monk Seal lives on the Atlantic coast of northwestern Africa as far south as Cap Blanc. Pups are born in October and November, mating takes place about two months after the pups are born. The Monk Seal is almost exclusively fish-eating and flounders seem to form the major part of its prey.

The northern coast of Iceland and the coast of Scandinavia from the White Sea to central Norway are home to the Hooded Seal (*Cystophora cristata*), an inhabitant of the northern Atlantic and Arctic Oceans. Rare stragglers have appeared off the British Isles. The male has a pouch of skin stretching from the muzzle up to the top of the head and connected to the nasal cavity (4). When the animal gets excited the pouch inflates to form a crest, the 'hood', on the head, about 20 cm high and almost 30 cm long. Young males do not develop this sac until their fourth year. Hooded Seals are solitary, only in the breeding season (March and April) will the male, the female and the pup stay together. The pup is suckled for only two weeks and its development is very rapid. When the pup is ready to be weaned the female mates again and leaves for the sea, while the young remain on the ice for another four weeks. The diet of the Hooded Seal consists of cephalopods (squids etc.) and fish. Remains of crustacea and starfish have been found in their stomachs which suggests that they also feed on the sea floor.

With the exception of the Monk Seal, the species referred to above are characterized by a marked sexual dimorphism, males being much larger than females.

	L (cm)		W (kg)	
	males	females	males	females
Halichoerus gryphus	250—330	180—250	180—320	130—230
Monachus monachus	230—280		250—300	
Cystophora cristata	210—250	180—200	260—300	145—160

4 ♂

1 ♂

2

♀

3

Red Squirrel
Sciurus vulgaris

Order: Rodentia
Family: Sciuridae

The Red Squirrel (1, 2) is widespread throughout Europe and the northern parts of Asia. Although it may be found in mixed woodland, it prefers coniferous forests. In the British Isles it is now found only in isolated populations, and is rare in central and southeastern England. In many cities of continental Europe, the Red Squirrel has become accustomed to the presence of man and is abundant in urban parks and gardens. The numbers of squirrels vary from year to year, one reason being the fluctuating yields of cones, nuts and seeds. Coniferous seeds, hazel nuts and acorns are the chief items in the Red Squirrel diet which also includes various fruits, the buds and bark of trees—mainly of young shoots—and mushrooms. Occasionally it will also take insects and rob bird's nests. It mostly looks for food in the trees, less often on the ground when it takes its food back up a tree or at least onto a high stump to eat. Squirrels store food for the winter either in hollow trees or in holes in the ground; however, they often cannot find their stores again. Squirrels build nests (dreys) for summer and winter. The summer dreys are usually built of green, leafy twigs, in the branches of a tree, and several dreys are built on the outskirts of each individual's home range. They serve as resting and sleeping places and also play an important part in marking the territory. In the winter and for rearing their young, squirrels build large nests close to the tree trunk. These dreys measure 30—40 cm across and have one (3) or more (4) entrances; sometimes a partition separates them into two. Breeding takes place twice a year, usually in February—March and in May—June. After a pregnancy of 35—40 days the female produces 3—7 young. These open their eyes at about 1 month old and leave their mother at around 8 weeks.

The Red Squirrel varies greatly in colour. Light red, black (1) and brownish-red (2) individuals may be encountered, all with an irregular white patch on their underparts. The short summer fur (2) is usually paler than the longer winter fur (1). In winter squirrels also develop long ear tufts and a much bushier tail. Squirrels in England and Ireland are reddish-brown with creamy-white underparts (5), in winter the coat is brownish-grey.

Britain is also the home of the Grey Squirrel (*Sciurus carolinensis*) (6, summer; 7, winter coat). This species, native to North America, was introduced into England in the last century and has become widespread in England and Wales, particularly in southern England. Isolated populations exist also in Scotland and Ireland. It has replaced the Red Squirrel in many areas and in this respect is an unwelcome intruder. Its diet is much more varied than that of the Red Squirrel and it seems to be more adaptable. Due to its predilection for tree buds and the bark of young shoots it can be a serious forest pest.

Its breeding season begins towards the end of December and ends in June. It usually produces two litters a year, each of 1—7 young. These are suckled for more than 2 months. In contrast to the Red Squirrel, the Grey Squirrel more often makes its nest in holes in trees or nest boxes. Young squirrels reared by hand are easily tamed.

	Lhb (mm)	Lt (mm)	W (g)
Sciurus vulgaris	180—270	140—200	200—400
S. carolinensis	230—300	200—250	500—570

Alpine Marmot
Marmota marmota

Order: Rodentia
Family: Sciuridae

The Alpine Marmot (1) is native to the Alps and the Carpathians but has also been introduced to the Pyrenees and to the northern parts of former Yugoslavia. It lives on grassy slopes and screes above the tree line, up to heights of about 2,500 m. It is rarely found lower down or at altitudes over 3,000 m. Family groups or small colonies occupy territories of around 1–3 hectares. The boundaries are marked by scent from the marmots' cheek glands which they rub on stones. Marmots dig deep burrows among stones which they line with dry grass for the winter (2), filling in the entrances with grass, earth and stones. They then settle down to spend the time from October to April in hibernation. As a rule, the whole family, or at least several individuals, hibernate together. They emerge from winter sleep towards the end of April or the beginning of May, depending on the weather. The rutting and mating season begins about a fortnight later and is accompanied by combats between males and wooing ceremonies (3). Pregnancy lasts 35–42 days and, in a burrow which is ordinarily shallower and shorter than a winter burrow, 2–6 young are born. Their eyes open at around 5 weeks and they do not leave the burrow before 2 months. Even then, however, they stay with their mother until the spring of the following year.

The Alpine Marmot is typically diurnal. As a rule, it never wanders far away from its burrow. One member of the colony is usually on guard and warns its fellow members of impending danger by a shrill whistle. The marmot is a herbivore which feeds mainly on various grasses and herbaceous plants and rummages for roots. Occasionally, it may add variety to its diet by taking birds' eggs.

The Bobac Marmot (*Marmota bobac*) (4) is an inhabitant of the steppes. It used to live in western Russia but its range has been pushed eastwards as these areas were exploited and it now survives in small isolated colonies round Kharkov, Rostov and Voronezh in the last, legally protected remains of the western steppe. Bobac Marmots are still abundant in central Asia as far as western China and southwards to northern India.

Its burrows (5) are very characteristic, and differ from those of other marmots. The earth excavated from the burrow is trampled down for 20—25 m around the entrance. At the centre, at the entrance to the burrow itself, the layer of earth may be 0.5—1 m thick. The ground near the burrow is kept free from vegetation. So Bobac Marmot colonies occupy large areas and it is easy to see how they could not survive as land was cultivated. Usually at the beginning of April, Bobac Marmots awaken from a winter sleep lasting 6—7 months and devote themselves to cleaning their burrows and excavating earth. This cleaning and excavating is repeated in July. Mating takes place immediately after leaving the burrows in spring, sometimes inside the burrow; if the latter, the female does not appear on the surface until after the young are born. Gestation takes around a month. There are usually 4—5 young in a litter but there is a high death rate and only about a half survive until autumn. Nevertheless, numbers may occasionally reach plague proportions, in which case females reproduce only once every 2 or 3 years until a balance is restored.

	Lhb (cm)	Lt (cm)	W (kg)
Marmota marmota	40—60	13—20	3—8
M. bobac	49—57	11—14	3—7

European Souslik or **Ground Squirrel**

Citellus citellus

Order: Rodentia
Family: Sciuridae

The European Souslik (1) is found in central and southeastern Europe, Asia Minor and the Near East. It lives in steppes, meadows and pastures, and cultivated fields. In the recent past, numbers have declined rapidly over the entire western part of its range, and it has disappeared altogether from many areas. This is primarily due to modern methods of cultivation which destroy the sousliks' habitat.

Sousliks live in colonies in burrows they dig themselves. Permanent burrows have a breeding chamber with two entrances, one sloping and the other leading vertically down (2). They also make simple temporary tunnels. Sousliks hibernate in the permanent burrows, filling the entrances with grass and earth. Older individuals fall into a winter sleep in August, sometimes as early as July. Young individuals go into hibernation later, usually in September. Depending on weather conditions, sousliks wake in March or April. They are active in the daytime, especially in the morning and early afternoon. Besides eating plants and seeds they catch insects and rob birds' nests. The mating period lasts from April to May. After a 25—28-day pregnancy 3—8 young, rarely more, are born. Their eyes open at 1 month. They are suckled for about 6 weeks, and by then they are already moving about the colony on their own.

The beautiful Spotted Souslik (*Citellus suslicus*) (3) inhabits the steppes stretching between the Volga and the Don and westwards as far as Poland and Rumania. Its life-style is very similar to that of the European Souslik but it is more often found in arable fields and digs longer, branching burrows. In the northern part of their range Spotted Sousliks often live singly in scattered burrows. They go into hibernation in August—September, in spring they emerge from their burrows towards the end of March or the beginning of April, and mate soon after. Pregnancy lasts 24—27 days and there are 2—12 young in a litter.

The Pygmy Souslik (*Citellus pygmaeus*) (4) is widespread from the Balkhash Lake westwards as far as the River Dnieper. It has been gradually migrating westwards in historical times and has only been stopped by the changes in the environment caused by cultivation. Thy Pygmy Souslik will also live in semi-desert and colonizes the margins of forest-steppes. Wherever it meets the Spotted Souslik, the latter has to give way. One reason is that the Pygmy Souslik is active at lower temperatures and is far more adaptable. The time of hibernation roughly coincides with the other species. Sometimes, however, in the hottest part of the year the Pygmy Souslik falls into a state of summer dormancy, called 'aestivation'. In some cases this merges into the deeper winter sleep. Mating occurs soon after waking up in spring. The gestation period is 25—26 days, each litter usually comprising 3—6 young.

	Lhb (mm)	Lt (mm)	W (g)
Citellus citellus	175—240	40—80	200—340
C. suslicus	180—230	30—45	170—340
C. pygmaeus	180—210	30—40	170—320

1

4

2

3

Flying Squirrel or Russian Flying Squirrel
Pteromys volans

Order: Rodentia
Family: Sciuridae

The westernmost limit of the Flying Squirrel (1) stretches through Finland and the Baltic States approximately along the line Ryazan—Kazan. Its range extends eastwards over Siberia as far as Japan. It is a typically shy nocturnal animal, living in mixed birch/alder forests. It is not particularly common anywhere and has become very rare in the western part of its range. It hides in holes in trees, occasionally in abandoned squirrel dreys, but never builds its own nest. Only rarely does it descend from the trees. Loose folds of skin on either side of the body enable it to glide for up to 40 m (2). It can even change direction by moving its limbs and steering with its tail. Its food is chiefly buds of various trees (e.g. maples, birches and alders) and it likes to gnaw young sprouts of both deciduous and coniferous trees. In summer it feeds on fruits. For the winter it gathers large stores of buds, particularly of birch and alder. There is little information on its reproduction: mating probably occurs in March and April. After a pregnancy of approximately a month, the female gives birth to 2—4 young. These are naked and blind; at 10 days their eyes open and fur starts to grow.

The Eutamias or Siberian Chipmunk (*Eutamias sibiricus*) (3) lives in the Siberian taiga but has been introduced to some regions of central and western Europe or formed feral populations there after having escaped from captivity. It is diurnal and extremely agile, and although an excellent climber, prefers to stay on the ground, where it feeds mainly on seeds. In August it starts storing supplies which it carries in its small cheek pouches. Large quantities (up to 3—4 kg) of seeds are sometimes gathered. Although the Eutamias has an interrupted winter sleep, its activity slows down and it does not leave its burrow. As a rule, a single pair hibernates in each burrow. They mate in March, immediately after emerging. After 35—40 days the female gives birth to 4—10 young.

The porcupines are interesting rodents of the family Hystricidae. North Africa is the home of the Crested or Common Porcupine (*Hystrix cristata*) (4) bearing a pale mane on the neck and dark quills at the base of the tail. It has also been introduced to southern Italy and Sicily. Porcupines are nocturnal and prefer thin woodland and wooded plains. They spend the day hiding in extensive burrows. Their diet chiefly consists of roots and bulbs, and the bark of trees and shrubs, but they also take animal food such as insects. The breeding period lasts from May to October and the female produces 1—3 litters a year. There are usually 2 young in a litter. No exact data are available on the duration of pregnancy: the shortest estimates are 65 days, the longest 112 days.

	Lhb (mm)	Lt (mm)	W
Pteromys volans	140—200	90—140	90—170 g
Eutamias sibiricus	120—170	80—115	50—120 g
Hystrix cristata	600—800	50—90	15—30 kg

European Beaver
Castor fiber

Order: Rodentia
Family: Castoridae

The European Beaver (1) was once very common throughout Europe and northern Asia, today it is extinct in many areas, for it has been hunted for its highly valued fur. About 150 years ago it disappeared from most of Europe, and it is only thanks to strict protection that it has been preserved in some regions along the Elbe and the Rhône, and also in northern Poland. It has been successfully reintroduced to Sweden, Norway, the Baltic Republics, and around the upper reaches of the Danube. In the past the beaver was common in Britain but was exterminated towards the end of the 12th century. It probably never lived in Ireland.

The beaver must live near water, and is well-adapted for its semi-aquatic life. Its small ears can be closed (just like nostrils), the fur is dense and the hindfeet are webbed. Two split claws on the second toes of the hindfeet are used to groom an oily secretion into the fur. The very characteristic tail is bare, flat and covered with scaly skin, and serves both as a paddle and a rudder when swimming (2). Beavers live in loose colonies of 12—15 members formed by family units. The basis of the family is a pair which stays together for life; they are joined by last year's and the current year's young. If colonies grow too big, the oldest pairs usually leave to found a new one. Where beavers are not disturbed, colonies can remain in existence for several hundred years. Besides burrows dug in the banks beavers construct 'lodges' made of branches, reeds and mud (4). Single lodges may be up to 1.5 m high and are reached through an underwater entrance. A permanent water level is secured by dams built of felled trees. Individual beaver ponds are interconnected by channels 30—60 cm deep made by a continuous use of pathways. Beavers need an enormous amount of timber for a new set of dams. Extraordinarily powerful incisors enable a beaver to fell trees as much as 70 cm in diameter. It usually fells trees with soft wood such as alders, poplars and willows, and gnaws through them in an extremely characteristic way (3). Beavers do not hibernate in winter but their activity is reduced and they stay in their lodge sometimes for several weeks, living on the bark of branches previously used as building material. They mate in January and February. After a pregnancy of 65—128 days the female gives birth to 2—6 young, already fully furred and with their eyes open. Though suckled for 6 weeks, the young take solid food without help at around a month old. Parents and young usually stay together for 2 years, which is the time needed for the young to reach sexual maturity.

The Canadian Beaver (*Castor canadensis*), which has a narrower head and shorter face (5, front part of the skull from above in *C. europaeus*; 6, in *C. canadensis*) has been successfully introduced to Finland.

The Coypu or Nutria (*Myocastor coypus*) (7), a representative of the family Myocastoridae, is indigenous to the non-tropical regions of South America. It has been reared for its fur in many European countries. From time to time escapees give rise to feral populations which may survive for several years. In East Anglia it has become a pest. Coypus are herbivorous, feeding on aquatic and waterside vegetation. Two litters of 5—6 young are born each year; the gestation period is around 128—132 days.

	Lhb (cm)	Lt (cm)	W (kg)
Castor fiber	75—100	30—40	13—35
Myocastor coypus	40—60	30—45	7—9 in the wild
			7—14 in farms

1

2

3

4

5

6

7

Common Hamster
Cricetus cricetus

Order: Rodentia
Family: Cricetidae

The Common Hamster (1) is found throughout most of Europe and Asia, from Siberia to Belgium and northeastern France. Originally an inhabitant of open grassland, it started spreading westward as Europe's forests gave way to fields and meadows. It makes deep burrows and so needs a soil cover more than 1 m deep. The hamster is a solitary animal active at dusk or at night. Although essentially herbivorous, it also catches insects and even smaller rodents. It stores food for the winter in its burrows, carrying it in capacious cheek pouches. Stores containing as much as 15 kg of food (grain, for example) are not uncommon. Hamsters hibernate between October and February and wake at intervals to eat the food they have stored, but never leave the burrows until April. The breeding season lasts from April to August. The female may produce three litters a year. After a pregnancy of 17—20 days 4—12 young are born. Their eyes open at 2 weeks and they then immediately leave the nest. They quickly reach maturity, with the young of the first litters being able to breed in the same year.

Radde's Golden Hamster (*Mesocricetus raddei*) (2) ranges from the eastern Caucasus over the Ukraine as far as Bulgaria and Rumania. Although it prefers dry grassland, it can also be found in cornfields. Its biology is similar to that of the Common Hamster. There are usually 2 litters a year, each with as many as 12 young. Closely related to Radde's Golden Hamster is the well-known Golden Hamster (*Mesocricetus auratus*) (3) which is not only commonly bred for laboratory purposes but also kept as a pet. It lives in the wild in Syria and Lebanon and its history is interesting. In 1930 Professor Aharoni of the Hebrew University in Jerusalem obtained eight young which he reared and subsequently presented to the pathology department of the University. Four escaped, one female died, but the remaining three individuals, one male and two females, reproduced successfully and all the Golden Hamsters bred today are their descendants. The gestation period is only 16 days and the young can breed at 7—8 weeks. Golden Hamsters have proved extremely useful as laboratory animals in medical research.

The Migratory or Grey Hamster (*Cricetulus migratorius*) (4) is very widespread in Asia, and its range extends across the Near East and Asia Minor westward to the Ukraine, Rumania, Bulgaria and Greece. Although originally a native of steppes and semi-deserts, it has developed a liking for human habitations. Migratory Hamsters are solitary animals, each digging its own burrow, but in the winter they often assemble to invade human settlements. Migratory Hamsters only hibernate in severe winters. Pregnancy lasts 20—21 days and there may be up to three litters of 3—10 young each year.

	Lhb (mm)	Lt (mm)	W (g)
Cricetus cricetus	220—340	28—60	150—600
Mesocricetus raddei	100—150	10—15	80—150
M. auratus	112—180	10—15	80—150
Cricetulus migratorius	87—120	20—30	25—36

Norway Lemming
Lemmus lemmus

Order: Rodentia
Family: Cricetidae

The Norway Lemming (1) lives in Scandinavia and the Kola Peninsula of Russia, inhabiting the subalpine zone of the mountain tundra. Under the grasses, mosses and lichens which cover the ground lemmings dig their tunnels interspersed with larger chambers where they eat their food. They move along these passages even in winter, under the snow. The lemmings' diet is predominantly mosses, bilberries and red whortleberries, the bark of goat willow and birches, grass and fungi. Lemmings reproduce all the year round, even in winter, producing as many as 7 litters a year. The gestation period is 20–21 days, with 3–7 young in each litter. Numbers of lemmings fluctuate from year to year. Years in which lemmings are very scarce are followed by 'lemming years' in which their numbers increase to plague proportions. These plague years recur regularly every three or four years, and are linked to marked increases in the species which feed on lemmings, such as Stoats, Arctic Foxes, Snowy Owls and Rough-legged Buzzards. Sometimes whole lemming populations set out in search of new territories. During population explosions these travelling lammings may join together to form large colonies and migrate very long distances, even to southern Scandinavia. Rivers and lakes present no obstacles as lemmings are good swimmers.

The Wood Lemming (*Myopus schisticolor*) (2) has a discontinuous distribution from Scandinavia over Siberia as far as Sakhalin. It lives in coniferous forests where it prefers damp places overgrown with *Sphagnum* moss. Wood Lemming populations are usually smaller than those of the Norway Lemming, and cyclic rises in populations and migrations are less frequent. The Wood Lemmings' diet consists almost exclusively of mosses and lichens. The female produces 1–3 litters a year, each of 3–5 young. Some years females constitute the major part of the population (up to 70 per cent).

The tundra belt stretching from the Kamchatka Peninsula in the east to Archangelsk in the west is the home of the Siberian Lemming (*Lemmus sibiricus*) (3). It is usually found in low-lying damp places overgrown with sallow, dwarf birches and grass. When the spring thaw comes it moves to higher ground. In good sites it forms large settled colonies living in complex burrows just beneath the surface. It can breed even in winter. 4–5 litters, usually of 5 young, are produced each year.

The Arctic or Collared Lemming (*Dicrostonyx torquatus*) is an inhabitant of the Arctic zone of Europe, Asia and North America, living on higher ground in the tundra. It chiefly feeds on willow and birch leaves and bark, on buds, berries and fungi. While the winter fur is almost pure white (4), the summer coat has a rusty hue and a white collar. In winter the claws on the 3rd and the 4th toes of the forefeet grow long and are used to dig in frozen ground and in hard snow. There are 2–3 litters of 4–6 young a year.

	Lhb (mm)	Lt (mm)	W (g)
Lemmus lemmus	130—150	15—20	35—130
Myopus schisticolor	85—125	12—20	15—40
Lemmus sibiricus	90—120	15—20	20—40
Dicrostonyx torquatus	130—140	20—23	35—135

Bank Vole
Clethrionomys glareolus

Order: Rodentia
Family: Cricetidae

The Bank Vole (1) inhabits the woodlands of Europe and Asia. It is abundant in mainland Britain and is found also on Skomer, Mull, Raasay and Jersey. Although it prefers deciduous and mixed forests, it may also be found in copses and hedgerows and sometimes in reed-beds. The burrows are dug just below the surface or in ground litter. It is mainly active at night but may often be seen running around in the daytime. In the first half of the year it feeds mainly on green plants, bark and seeds, in summer and autumn it also takes beechmast and acorns, nuts and fungi, and also insects. Breeding starts as early as March and even in February in warm weather. In good mast years Bank Voles multiply even in winter. From March to October the female may produce up to 4 litters, giving birth to 3—6 young after a pregnancy of 18—21 days. The young leave the nest at about 3 weeks and can breed soon after. Cyclic population explosions of Bank Voles recur at intervals of around 3 to 5 years. In these plague years they can do considerable damage by biting off young shoots and seedlings (2), and being excellent climbers, they can reach a height of several metres.

The range of the Large-toothed Red-backed or Grey-sided Vole (*Clethrionomys rufocanus*) (4) extends from northern Norway to the Far East. Its typical habitat is the taiga, the sparse northern woodland, but it also occurs in the tundra and spreads along river valleys into the coniferous forest. Buds and shoots of dwarf birches and willows make up its diet and otherwise its biology resembles that of the Bank Vole.

The Northern or Ruddy Red-backed Vole (*Clethrionomys rutilus*) (5) is an inhabitant of the Arctic zone of Asia and North America, just reaching northern Scandinavia. Its home is the coniferous forest, but in the far north it lives on the tundra, and in the south it has spread into the forest-steppe where it mostly colonizes birch woodland. It lives on seeds, fruits and plant parts but in winter often moves into buildings. The female usually produces 3—4 litters a year, each of 7—8 young.

When they eat nuts, members of the genus *Clethrionomys* hold the shell close to their body. Resting their upper incisors on the inner side of the shell, they use their lower incisors to gnaw the shell from the outside, leaving no scratches on the surface (3).

The Sagebrush Vole (*Lagurus lagurus*) (6) lives on the steppe and semi-desert, and also in wooded grassland from the River Dnieper to central Asia. It also colonizes pastureland, and spreading along roadsides, it may even reach intensively farmed areas. The Sagebrush Vole digs burrows with three or four entrances, piling up the excavated earth around the main central entrance into a little oval mound. A slanting tunnel joins the main entrance to the nest chamber which is usually 20—30 cm below the surface and lined with soft grass. The parents share the burrow until the birth of the young. The male then leaves to live in a simple temporary burrow. The female may produce as many as 6 litters a year of 3—7 young. Since the gestation period is around 15—23 days and the young take only 20—25 days to mature, population explosions are fairly common.

	Lhb (mm)	Lt (mm)	W (g)
Clethrionomys glareolus	80—120	30—67	10—40
C. rufocanus	100—130	28—40	15—55
C. rutilus	80—110	23—35	15—40
Lagurus lagurus	90—114	9—13	13—35

116

Water Vole
Arvicola terrestris

Order: Rodentia
Family: Cricetidae

The Water Vole (1, 2, 4) lives in central and eastern Europe, and here and there throughout western Europe. Eastwards it is found throughout northern Asia as far as the Pacific coast, and in mountains it may appear farther south. It is found in mainland Britain, the Isle of Wight and Anglesey, where it is most frequently found along overgrown banks of rivers and lakes. In the autumn, Water Voles may often be encountered far from water, in gardens and orchards. Some prefer to live in this way all the year round, never returning to the waterside. Water Voles are secretive and we are more likely to find their traces rather than see the animals themselves. In spring and summer, Water Voles mostly feed on grass and leaves, gnawing off aquatic plants even underwater. In autumn and winter, they chiefly eat roots and can cause damage to young plantations. They store small amounts of food in their burrows for the winter when they do not come out onto the surface. The breeding season lasts from March to October. After a pregnancy of 18—21 days, the female gives birth to 4—6 young in a nest in an underground burrow. In a single year she may produce three or four litters. The young start swimming at 12 days and at 6—8 weeks they can breed. In the breeding season males have conspicuous scent glands on their sides, which they use for marking their territory.

A very similar species inhabiting the Iberian Peninsula and the greater part of western Europe is the Dwarf Fruit-eating Vole (*Arvicola sapidus*) (3). It is somewhat larger, with a longer tail, and also differs in some features of the skull. In some areas both species live side by side, but the Dwarf Fruit-eating Vole is never found too far away from water.

The Muskrat (*Ondatra zibethicus*) (5, 6) lives on overgrown river banks. In thick mud it is possible to find the distinctly outlined prints of its long hindpaws (8) and short forepaws (7). Its original home is North America and it was introduced to Europe early this century for its fur. Today, it is found sporadically eastwards from France as far as China. Muskrats usually live in pairs. They either excavate burrows in river banks or live in lodges of reed built in shallow water (9), which in winter serve also as food. At least one entrance to the burrow or lodge is under water. Breeding takes place from April to September. After a pregnancy of 28 days the female gives birth to 5—7 young. There are usually 3—4 litters each year. The young develop into perfect swimmers and divers at the early age of 3 weeks. Muskrat fur (musquash) is highly prized and the animals are intensively hunted. They are chiefly herbivorous, complementing their diet with aquatic molluscs.

	Lhb (mm)	Lt (mm)	W (g)
Arvicola terrestris	120—200	80—130	60—200
A. sapidus	170—220	100—140	100—300
Ondatra zibethicus	250—400	190—290	800—1,600

European Pine Vole
Pitymys subterraneus

Order: Rodentia
Family: Cricetidae

The range of the European Pine Vole (1) extends from northwestern France to the Ukraine and from the Baltic to the Balkan Peninsula. Its typical habitats are relatively damp, open areas and thin woodland with a good herbaceous understorey. Populations are discontinuous as it needs to live on lighter soils. It usually lives in small colonies, and individuals never leave the immediate vicinity of their burrows. The Pine Vole is a strict herbivore with a particular liking for leaves and stems; less often it takes seeds, fruits and fungi. In bad weather, in heavy rain or snow it fills up the entrances to its burrows. It is active in daytime but because it spends more time underground than other voles it is seldom encountered. The breeding season lasts from February until September. The gestation period is 20—23 days, and 3 litters of 2—4 young are usually produced each year. The females only have two pairs of teats. The young are cared for not only by their mother but by other individuals living in the colony and sharing the same nest.

The home of the Mediterranean Pine or Iberian Root Vole (*Pitymys duodecimostatus*) (2) is the Iberian Peninsula and southern France. Its biology closely resembles that of the Pine Vole but it is predominantly nocturnal and the burrows are surrounded with excavated earth. Differentiating features are the teeth (3, *P. subterraneus*; 4, *P. duodecimostatus*).

Savi's Pine or Mediterranean Root Vole (*Pitymys savii*) (5) is found in Apennine Italy and Sicily. In the opinion of some zoologists it also occurs in western France and in the south of the Balkan Peninsula. Some experts recognize nine species of the genus *Pitymys* in Europe, some of which are indistinguishable morphologically. They can be distinguished by the number, shape and size of their chromosomes. Some of these species have a very restricted area of distribution.

Voles of the genus *Pitymys* may at first sight be confused with the Mediterranean or Guenther's Vole (*Microtus guentheri*) (6). It is found throughout the Balkan Peninsula, Asia Minor and the Near East, as well as in eastern Libya where it inhabits dry plains and pastureland. Guenther's Vole is mainly nocturnal and lives in colonies. Individuals dig branched tunnel systems with numerous exits and a nesting chamber lined with dry grass, usually situated about 20 cm below the surface. The breeding season is in spring and autumn. From May until the end of July Guenther's Voles are usually sterile as the male's testicles are drawn into the body. Each litter has 6 young on average, but litters of 14 and even 17 have been reported. The young attain maturity at the age of 25—30 days, and the gestation period is 18—23 days. It is therefore not surprising that population explosions occasionally occur.

	Lhb (mm)	Lt (mm)	Lhp (mm)	W (g)
Pitymys subterraneus	80—105	24—32	14—16	13—25
P. duodecimostatus	85—105	20—30	15—18	14—23
P. savii	82—105	21—35	14—16	13—25
Microtus guentheri	86—135	20—40	16—22	30—60

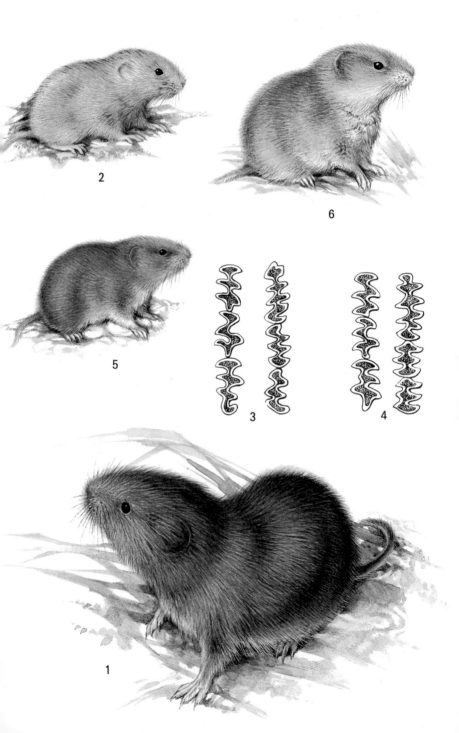

2

6

5

3   4

1

Field Vole
Microtus arvalis

Order: Rodentia
Family: Cricetidae

The Field Vole (1) is widespread throughout Europe except in Scandinavia, mainland Britain and the western Mediterranean countries. It is also found in the Orkneys, on Westray and Guernsey. Its range extends eastwards as far as China. It is a typical inhabitant of steppe grassland, but owing to its great adaptability, it is encountered everywhere, except deep in the forest. It is especially active at night, resting for longer periods during the day. The Field Vole lives in colonies conspicuous by their well-trodden pathways interconnecting the separate burrows. But there is no stable social system as individuals are not particularly sociable. The nest is usually located at the centre of a tunnel system, 10—20 cm below the surface. The nesting chamber is lined with dry grass woven into a spherical nest. There are also short burrows for temporary protection against danger which are also used to eat in. In favourable conditions the Field Vole may breed all the year round. Up to 6 litters of 4—7 young are produced each year. Gestation takes 19—21 days. After reaching sexual maturity at the early age of 3—5 weeks the young start breeding. Field Voles have cycles of population explosion every 3—5 years. Lack of food as well as disease and stress then contribute to a rapid decline in numbers. The grinding surface of the molars is illustrated in (2).

The Short-tailed Vole (*Microtus agrestis*) (5) is found in mainland Britain, the Hebrides, Orkneys and the Channel Islands across central Europe as far as central Siberia, but is absent from most of the Mediterranean. The Short-tailed Vole differs from the very similar Field Vole not only in certain body dimensions and in the shape of the molars (3), but also by the dark soles to its hindfeet. It prefers damper and cooler habitats and also lives in woodland. Unlike the Field Vole it builds its nest above ground. Females give birth from May to October. Pregnancy takes 19—21 days, and litters usually comprise 4—6 young.

The Tundra Vole (*Microtus oeconomus*) (6) greatly resembles the Short-tailed Vole. Its discontinuous distribution extends over the tundra and taiga of Europe and Asia. Isolated populations are found in northern Germany, the Netherlands and the great Hungarian plain, and in southern Slovakia. It favours damp places, marshes and reed-beds, and has a diet of marsh plants. The grass-lined nest is usually built above ground — often, for example, in a tuft of sedge. The breeding season starts in March and ends in November. There are two or three litters of 2—9 young a year. Pregnancy lasts 20—23 days.

The Snow or Alpine Vole (*Microtus nivalis*) (7) inhabits the mountain ranges of Europe and also occurs in the Caucasus and the Near East. Its favourite habitats are screes and mountain meadows, usually above the timberline. It lives in colonies but does not dig burrows, mostly hiding in rock crevices or between stones. It lives on plants, berries and seeds. Breeding is confined to May—August, and no more than 2 litters of 1—5 young are produced each year. These mature after emerging from hibernation. The grinding surfaces of the molars (4) are characteristic.

	Lhb (mm)	Lt (mm)	Lhp (mm)	W (g)
Microtus arvalis	80—130	20—50	13—18.5	15—50
M. agrestis	90—140	28—52	16—21	16—60
M. oeconomus	98—140	38—74	16—23	20—60
M. nivalis	85—140	40—75	19—22	35—65

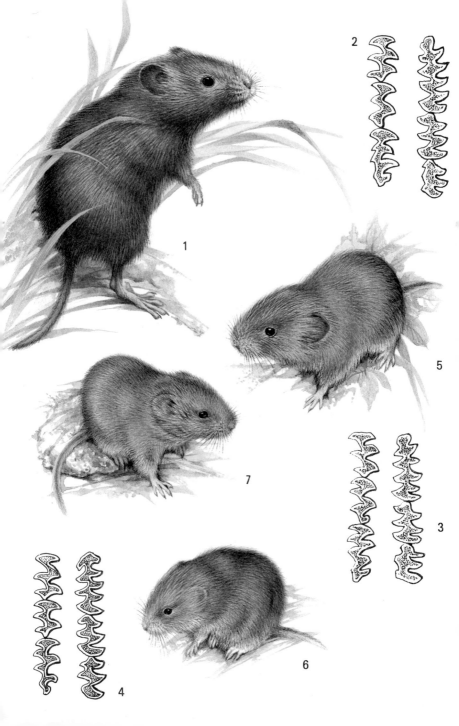

Lesser Mole Rat
Spalax leucodon

Order: Rodentia
Family: Spalacidae

The Lesser Mole Rat (1) lives in Hungary, spreading over the Balkan Peninsula to Asia Minor and over Transcaucasia to the western Ukraine. It inhabits grassy steppes as well as cultivated land and pastureland, and occasionally open woodland. In the limestone (karst) areas of the Balkans it is most frequently found in limestone bores. The Lesser Mole Rat spends practically all its life in its underground tunnel system, only occasionally emerging above ground to bask in the sun near the burrow. It is perfectly adapted to its underground, burrowing way of life, with a cylindrical tailless body, no external ears, and vestigial eyes completely hidden under the skin. It loosens the earth with its powerful incisors, and uses its head, which is armed with a horny nose plate and a row of tough bristles on either side, to remove the loosened earth from the burrows. At the centre of the tunnel system is a large mound of excavated earth with a nursery nest underneath. Smaller mounds connected to the nest by tunnels are placed along the boundary of the territory. In summer they serve the Lesser Mole Rats as resting nests. Lesser Mole Rats are herbivores which feed on roots, tubers and bulbs. From November to January, when the mating season sets in, these otherwise solitary animals form groups. Peripheral mounds are often inhabited by single males who court the female residing in the nest. The gestation period is about 28 days. The first litters are brought forth in February, the second from the end of March till May. There are, as a rule, 2—4 young in a litter — rarely up to 9.

The Greater or Russian Mole Rat (*S. microphthalmus*) (2), a native of the Ukraine, extends eastward to the westernmost part of Siberia, southward to the Caucasus, and is possibly also native to Rumania and Greece. It resembles *S. leucodon* in its way of life. The skulls of both the Greater (3) and the Lesser (4) Mole Rat are wedge-shaped, with a conspicuously broad nape region.

The Mole Lemming (*Ellobius talpinus*) (5) has a similar life-style, although it belongs to the hamster family (Cricetidae). It is found in steppes and semi-deserts from the Ukraine over Crimea to Turkestan and eastward as far as Mongolia. Like mole rats, it uses its strong front teeth to dig two-storied burrows. In the tunnels situated close to the surface Mole Lemmings search for food, while in the lower tunnels they build their nests. Characteristic earth mounds at the burrow entrance are made by the Mole Lemming throwing the loosened earth backward with its hindlegs (6). Roots and bulbs form its diet. Mole Lemmings breed all the year round and usually produce 3—4 litters a year of 2—4 young. Gestation takes 26—28 days.

	Lhb (mm)	Lt (mm)	Lhp (mm)	W (g)
Spalax leucodon	150—270	—	20—25	140—220
S. microphthalmus	197—300	—	24—30	370—570
Ellobius talpinus	100—120	8—15	19—23	20—50

Yellow-necked Mouse
Apodemus flavicollis

Order: Rodentia
Family: Muridae

The Yellow-necked Mouse (1) is found in most of southern England and Wales and throughout Europe from eastern France to the Urals. The northernmost limit of its range is southern Scandinavia; in the south it occurs in the Pyrenees, Italy and the Balkan Peninsula, and in the Near East. It is nocturnal and a typical inhabitant of all types of woodland, hedgerows and gardens. Long hindlegs enable it to make long jumps and it is a skilful climber. Its nests of grass and leaves are built between stones or tree roots, not infrequently even in nest-boxes. Seeds constitute the bulk of its diet, supplemented with insects, slugs and other small invertebrates. Yellow-necked Mice hoard seeds for the winter. They breed from February to September and, if the weather is good, throughout the winter. Reproduction also depends on the food supply. The female gives birth to 2—9 young after a pregnancy of 23—29 days.

The Wood Mouse or Long-tailed Field Mouse (*A. sylvaticus*) (2) is very similar and even an expert can find it difficult to distinguish young individuals and females of the two species. A relatively reliable identifying feature is the length of the hindpaw, which is greater in *A. flavicollis*. The Wood Mouse is widespread throughout Europe, including mainland Britain and many of the islands, but is absent from northern Scandinavia. In Asia it extends as far as the Himalayas, in northwestern Africa it is rare. In the British Isles it is abundant, especially in the lowlands, inhabiting woodland edges, copses, reed-beds, hedgerows and open country, but avoiding thick woodland. It is nocturnal, with a very similar life-style to the Yellow-necked Mouse, but is less agile, less apt to climb, and more often digs burrows and builds underground nests. Its diet includes a considerable proportion of grass and herb seeds. The Wood Mouse does not often breed in winter and the number of young in a litter is usually 5.

The Pygmy Wood Mouse (*Apodemus microps*) (3) is very similar to the eastern form of the House Mouse or to a young Wood Mouse and was identified only in 1952. It is widespread in the Czech Republic, Slovakia, Poland, and southeastern Europe, and probably also in the Near East, inhabiting dry open country. Seeds of grasses, cereals and weeds form most of its diet, and it digs tunnels. Breeding takes place from March till September. Gestation takes about 23 days, and there are usually 2-6 young in each litter – frequently more.

The largest field mouse is the Broad-toothed Field Mouse or Rock Mouse (*Apodemus mystacinus*) (4) from southeastern Europe (the Adriatic coast of former Yugoslavia, the southern part of the Balkan Peninsula, eastern Mediterranean islands) and the Near East. It favours rocky and scrubby habitats where it shelters in rock crevices and does not dig burrows. The young mostly appear from April to September, with around 4-6 in a litter.

Nuts eaten by field mice can be recognized by the ring of minute scratches left by the upper incisors on the outside of the shell (5). The mouse holds the nut at an angle and rather far away from the body, using its lower incisors to gnaw at the inside of the shell.

	Lhb (mm)	Lt (mm)	Lhp (mm)	W (g)
Apodemus flavicollis	90—123	87—130	23—27	18—50
A. sylvaticus	75—110	70—110	19—24	15—38
A. microps	70—96	62—85	17—21	12—22
A. mystacinus	85—150	100—144	23—29	28—56

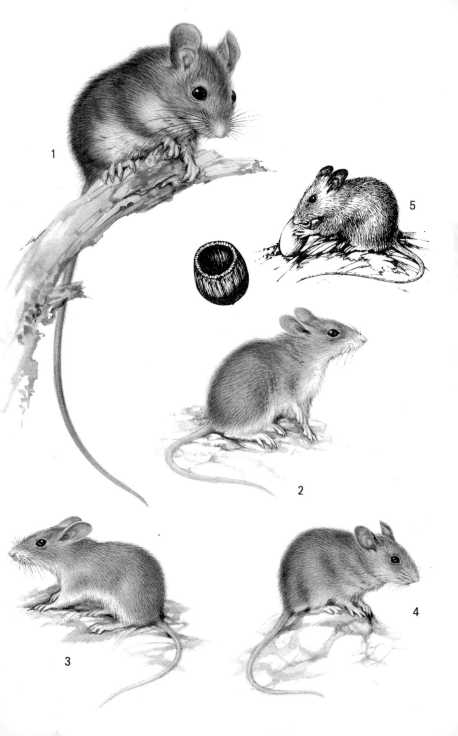

Striped Field Mouse
Apodemus agrarius

Order: Rodentia
Family: Muridae

The Striped Field Mouse (1) is distinguished by a dark stripe about 2—3 mm wide running from the top of its head along the back to the base of the tail. It lives in northern central Europe and in southeastern Europe from where its range extends over the Caucasus and central Siberia to the Far East. Damp river banks, thickets, dense undergrowth and other damp overgrown sites are its favourite habitats. It lives in families or small groups and digs shallow burrows with nesting and storage chambers. In winter it often comes into buildings, or colonizes woodstacks etc. The Striped Field Mouse is chiefly a seed-eater, but almost a third of its diet is made up of insects and their larvae. The breeding season is shorter than in other field mice, lasting only from April to September. Within this period the female may produce 2—3 litters of 4—9 young. Gestation lasts 21—23 days. In the eastern part of their range, Striped Field Mice may produce up to 5 litters a year, which leads to frequent population explosions. On these occasions, considerable damage may be done to field crops.

Spiny mice, members of the genus *Acomys,* are particularly interesting representatives of the family Muridae. Their name derives from the soft bristles on their backs, particularly conspicuous at the rear. Here they stick out from the rest of the normal fur. They also have an extremely fragile, easily detachable tail. There are several species, all very similar, found in Africa, Asia and around the Mediterranean. The Cairo Spiny Mouse (*Acomys cahirinus*) (2) lives in North and East Africa, the Egyptian Spiny Mouse (*Acomys dimidiatus*) (3) is found from Egypt to southeastern Asia, and on Cyprus and Crete. The two species can be distinguished by the shape of the skull and are also somewhat different in their lifestyle, the Egyptian Spiny Mouse preferring rocky sites. A third species, the Golden Spiny Mouse (*Acomys russatus*), ranges from eastern Egypt across Arabia as far as the Near East. It can easily be distinguished by the black soles to both hind- and forepaws, and by its distinctly rusty colouring. Spiny mice live in scrubby grassland, dry stony slopes and rocky places, often coming into buildings where they are easily caught. They are seed-eaters but also take insects and snails. The female gives birth to 2—3 well-developed young after a pregnancy of 35—37 days. Their eyes open as early as the second day, and at 1 week they can already fend for themselves. Mothers help each other with the birth and also often share the care of the young.

	Lhb (mm)	Lt (mm)	Lhp (mm)	W (g)
Apodemus agrarius	70—125	65—89	17—21	12—39
A. cahirinus	90—125	80—110	17—20	30—70
A. dimidiatus	94—128	90—120	18—22	35—86
A. russatus	94—128	89—120	18—20	30—85

Harvest Mouse

Micromys minutus

Order: Rodentia
Family: Muridae

The Harvest Mouse (1) is one of the smallest European rodents. It has small ears, a short, blunt snout, and a nearly naked, extraordinarily mobile tail almost equal in length to the body. The coat always has a yellowish hue — in summer it is pale, in winter a darker brown, sharply contrasting with the white underparts. The skull (3) has a relatively large brain case. The Harvest Mouse is found mainly in southern and eastern England and the Welsh borders, becoming rare further north. Its range extends throughout most of Europe, except the Iberian Peninsula and southern Italy, and on through Asia to the Far East and southwards as far as northern India. It likes damp places such as reed-beds, damp meadows and riverside woods, but also comes into fields in summer and autumn to eat ripe grain, and colonizes barns and haystacks. It is active during the day but easily escapes notice as it is extremely shy. Making use of its prehensile tail, it climbs the leaves and stems of grasses and cereal crops. The round nests, woven of grass, are built above ground, and usually have two openings. Large nests with a single opening are used for breeding (2). Nests are used in summer only, in winter the Harvest Mouse leaves them for underground burrows, where it sometimes stores modest food supplies. Seeds form the greater part of its diet, but insects are also important. The Harvest Mouse breeds from March-April to September and may produce up to 7 litters a year; however, 2—3 litters are more usual. The gestation period is 21 days, a litter usually comprising 3—7 young. Newborn young weigh no more than 0.6—0.8 g but grow rapidly. At 4 days old fur develops, their eyes open at 8—10 days, and at 11—12 days they are ready to leave the nest for the first time. They become sexually mature at 6 weeks.

The Striped Grass Mouse (*Lemniscomys barbarus*) (4) is an inhabitant of the dry plains and scrubland bordering the Sahara, being found as far as east Africa. It is solitary although the population density is usually relatively high, about 12 individuals per hectare. The Striped Grass Mouse is active day and night, making short raids for food early in the morning and in the evening. It is omnivorous and eats green plants, seeds, fruit, insects, and other invertebrates. The breeding period coincides with the rainy season. The female usually produces 4 litters of 4—5 young (sometimes up to 12) a year. Gestation takes 28 days. The young remain blind for about a week, then their eyes open and they develop rapidly. Although the young are sexually mature at 2 months, they do not breed until the following year.

	Lhb (mm)	Lt (mm)	Lhp (mm)	W (g)
Micromys minutus	50—77	40—75	12—16	3.5—12
Lemniscomys barbarus	90—118	95—133	22—26	33—41

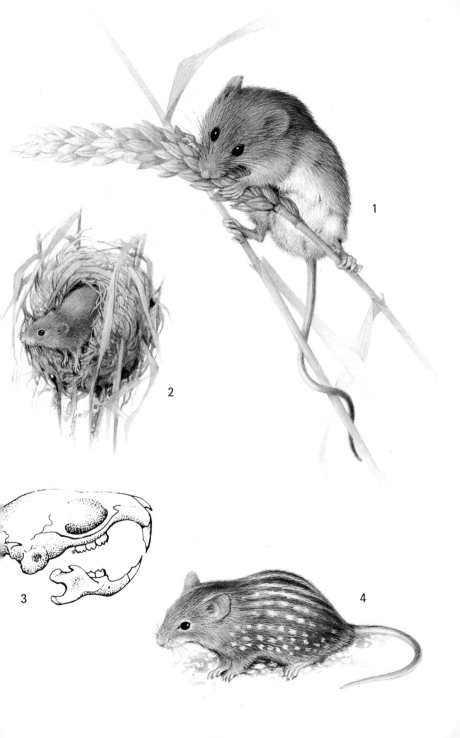

1

2

3

4

House Mouse
Mus musculus

Order: Rodentia
Family: Muridae

The House Mouse is originally a native of the warm grasslands of central Europe and Asia but has been introduced by man to all other parts of the world. It was brought to Britain in Roman times and is now found everywhere, living usually in close relationship with man, but also in the wild. The House Mouse is a very variable species and its variability is greatly influenced by the environment in which it lives. In general, western European House Mice are darker than their eastern counterparts, and the length of the tail also tends to decrease going west to east. The western European form, *Mus musculus domesticus* (1), occurs in Europe west of the River Elbe, almost exclusively in association with man. To the east, and in Scandinavia, the central European form, *Mus musculus musculus* (2), also lives with man. Feral House Mouse populations from southeastern Europe, which live in fields and only come into buildings sometimes in winter, are classed as the Eastern House Mouse, *Mus musculus spicilegus* (3), which is sometimes regarded as a separate species. House Mice living in and around buildings usually do not dig burrows but shelter in crevices in walls, in refuse heaps, and below floors. Here they also build their nests, mostly using paper and cloth as building material. Feral populations dig shallow, simple burrows in which they make nests of grass. Near the burrows they build store chambers which at first sight resemble molehills, and may be up to 50 cm high, 60—120 cm in diameter, and may contain up to 10 kg of grains and grass or corn ears. A labyrinth of tunnels and chambers open into the store chamber (4). House Mice living in buildings breed throughout the year, feral populations only from spring till autumn. The number of litters per year ranges from 5 to 10. A litter usually contains 4—9 young. The gestation period is 19—20 days. As a rule, mating occurs shortly after the female gives birth. The young mature and can breed at the age of 45 days. With this reproduction capacity, large and, on occasion, very damaging population explosions may take place.

The Iberian Peninsula, the Balearic Islands and northwestern Africa are the home of the Algerian House Mouse (*Mus spretus*) (5). Its life-style is similar to that of the eastern form of the House Mouse, but it is less gregarious and does not build store chambers.

The House Mouse has given rise to a great number of colour varieties bred as pets and laboratory animals. The oldest and most common is the white mouse. This was originally bred in China and Japan and was introduced from Japan to Europe 120 years ago.

	Lhb (mm)	Lt (mm)	Lhp (mm)	W (g)
Mus musculus domesticus	80—100	90—102	17—19	16—25
M. m. musculus	70—85	65—75	15—17	14—20
M. m. spicilegus	70—86	55—73	15—18	10—19
M. spretus	67—88	52—74	15—17	10—15

3

4

1

2

5

Black or Ship Rat
Rattus rattus

Order: Rodentia
Family: Muridae

Rat populations living in the wild are found in southeastern Asia (which is their original natural home), southern Europe and north Africa. Travelling on ships, the Black Rat was carried world-wide and was introduced to Europe, it is thought, some 3,000 years ago, and to Britain in the 12th century. In many areas it has now been replaced by the much more adaptable and prolific Brown Rat, and in Britain is now confined to relatively few locations. As with the House Mouse, it is very variable in size and colour. Within Europe, differently coloured individuals frequently appear even in a single litter. In central Europe it is most usually greyish-black and is designated *Rattus rattus rattus* (1). Southern Europe and the eastern parts of the Mediterranean are the home of somewhat larger rats whose colour is more brownish with grey underparts — *Rattus rattus alexandrinus* (2). In the western Mediterranean smaller, brownish, usually white-bellied rats are found — *Rattus rattus frugivorus* (3). Populations living in towns, particularly in seaports, are usually of all types of colouring. Rats climb and are often found in the top stories of buildings, in grain stores and in other dry places. Around the Mediterranean, feral rat populations can be found far away from human habitations, often living in trees. Rats living in the wild eat seeds, fruits and greenstuff, whereas rats near human habitations are omnivorous scavengers eating any scraps they can find. In buildings, rats build nests of paper and cloth, often in attics or in roof spaces, in the wild, nests of grass and leaves are built in shrubs or trees, often 2—5 m above the ground. Breeding continues all the year round. After a pregnancy of 21—23 days the female produces a litter of 7—8 young.

The Brown or Norwegian Rat (*Rattus norvegicus*) (4) is indigenous to eastern Asia but it has spread world-wide. It prefers a mild or cool climate, being considerably less common in subtropical or tropical regions. It has, however, colonized some islands (e.g. Madagascar), where it has caused immense and irreparable damage by destroying large numbers of the rare original fauna. In Europe the first mass increase in Brown Rat populations took place in the 18th century, and was largely due to the introduction of sewer systems in towns. Unlike the Black Rat, the Brown Rat prefers a damp environment, is a good swimmer, and in buildings mostly lives in cellars or the ground-floor. Here and there, feral Brown Rat populations may be encountered along watersides, or depending on a special food source. In contrast to Black Rats, Brown Rats dig burrows to live in. They breed throughout the year. The female usually gives birth to 6—10 young after a pregnancy of 22—24 days. Depending on living conditions, between 3 and 5 litters a year are produced. The young mature early, at 3 months, which makes this species very prolific. Brown Rat populations in towns often pose considerable public health and environmental problems.

	Lhb (mm)	Lt (mm)	Lhp (mm)	W (g)
Rattus rattus	160—235	186—250	39—40	135—250
R. norvegicus	160—270	125—230	30—45	140—500

Edible, Fat or Squirrel-tailed Dormouse
Glis glis

Order: Rodentia
Family: Gliridae

The Edible Dormouse (1) is native to most of Europe, being absent only in the northwest, northern Scandinavia, the Iberian Peninsula and the British Isles (here, however, it was introduced to Tring Park in Hertfordshire in 1902). Its range extends eastwards to Transcaucasia and southwards to the Near East.

The Edible Dormouse prefers deciduous forests, but also lives in gardens and parks, sometimes making an appearance in vineyards. It thrives on warm sunny slopes, and around the Mediterranean it frequently occurs in scrubby limestone areas. It is nocturnal, searching for food mainly in the trees. It lives in families, hiding by day in holes and rock crevices, and may even take over nest-boxes. It hibernates either in underground nests or in lofts. In the autumn it becomes very fat and towards the end of September or beginning of October it falls into a winter sleep (2) from which it emerges towards the end of April, often in May, and when the weather is bad, as late as June. Its diet varies with the seasons, in spring including buds, bark, green plants and small animals, in summer, seeds and fruit, and in autumn, fruit, acorns and beechnuts. Dormice mate soon after awakening from hibernation. The gestation period is 30—32 days. There are usually 3—6 young in a litter. They are suckled for about 1 month, at 2 months they can start fending for themselves. The skull of the Edible Dormouse has large tympanic hollows, the lower jaw is closed, without an opening at the angular projection (5). Skulls of all dormouse species are very similar.

The Common, British or Hazel Dormouse (*Muscardinus avellanarius*) (3) has a similar distribution to the Edible Dormouse, but is also found in southern England and Wales, in the Near East, and eastward as far as the Volga basin. It prefers damp sites and deciduous woodland with dense undergrowth, especially of hazel, but may also be found in purely coniferous forests and in the mountains in the Mountain Pine belt. The Common Dormouse comes out at twilight or night and often remains in shrubs and trees. It lives on a mixed diet, around one half formed of buds, bark, leaves, flowers and fruits, and the other half of insects, snails, earthworms, etc. Common Dormice usually settle down for hibernation at the beginning of September, younger ones rather later. They spend the winter under leaf litter or in holes, and usually wake in April. Each individual builds several summer nests, alternatively used for resting and sleeping, and also for breeding. The spherical nests are made of grass and leaves, often intertwined with shreds of bark (4). They may be situated in raspberry or hazel copses, or on the ground. Mating usually occurs in May; after a pregnancy of 23 days a litter of 3—5 young is produced. The Common Dormouse may produce up to two litters a year. Even though it is still common in some areas in Europe, it is seldom encountered due to its retired nocturnal life.

	Lhb (mm)	Lt (mm)	Lhp (mm)	W (g)
Glis glis	120—200	110—190	23—35	70—250
Muscardinus avellanarius	60—85	55—82	14—17	15—28

Garden or Oak Dormouse
Eliomys quercinus

Order: Rodentia
Family: Gliridae

The Garden Dormouse (1) is found scattered across Europe with the exception of Britain, Scandinavia and the coasts of the North and Baltic Seas. It ranges across the former USSR as far as the Urals, and is also found in North Africa. It lives in woodlands, gardens and orchards, where it spends much of its time on the ground looking for food. The summer nests are built of twigs, leaves and grass, sited in trees and shrubs or on the ground, mostly among stones, in old walls, etc. In spring and summer, the Garden Dormouse eats various invertebrates, and hunts small mammals and birds whose nests it robs. In the autumn it feeds on fruits and seeds. Several individuals usually hibernate together from October to April, sharing winter nests which they build in holes, rock crevices, or in underground burrows abandoned by other rodents. Soon after awakening from hibernation they mate, and after a gestation of 23 days a litter of 3—5 young is born. A single litter, rarely two, is produced each year.

The Forest Dormouse (*Dryomys nitedula*) (2) ranges from Switzerland and northern Italy over the Balkan Peninsula and the Carpathians as far as the Caucasus, and through central Asia to China. It prefers woodlands of all types, with a thick undergrowth. Its spherical summer nests are most often found in holes, nest-boxes, sometimes even in rock crevices and underground burrows. In the northern parts of its range it spends the winter in hibernation, which begins in October and ends in April. It hibernates in holes in trees or more often underground, about 30—60 cm below the surface. The southern populations remain active throughout the year. Its biology is not very different from that of the Garden Dormouse, but it has a more vegetarian diet. The Forest Dormouse breeds once or twice a year. The female is pregnant for 23—25 days and usually produces 2—6 young in each litter.

The Mouse-like or Ognev's Dormouse (*Myomimus roachi*) (3) was identified in southeastern Bulgaria. Unlike other dormice, it lives almost exclusively on the ground in the steppes. Its diet consists predominantly of seeds, and to a lesser extent of green plants. This very shy and retiring animal is probably extremely rare. We know next to nothing about its biology. It hides among stones and in underground burrows but does not do much digging itself.

In all dormice, the grinding surfaces of both premolars and molars have transverse ridges (4) which are characteristic for each species.

	Lhb (mm)	Lt (mm)	Lhp (mm)	W (g)
Eliomys quercinus	100—180	90—129	22—30	50—180
Dryomys nitedula	77—110	60—95	18—23	17—32
Myomimus roachi	90—130	60—80	18—22	15—25

Northern Birch Mouse
Sicista betulina

Order: Rodentia
Family: Zapodidae

The Northern Birch Mouse (1) is an inhabitant of the forests and forest plains of Europe and Asia, extending from Scandinavia to central Siberia and southward as far as the Caucasus. It is scattered throughout central Europe in various mountain ranges. It prefers moist localities with plenty of cover, peat-bogs, mountain meadows and pastures. It is equally at home on the ground and climbing, making use of its long prehensile tail. Its spherical nests of grass and moss are sited in holes, grass tufts, ferns, underneath bark, etc. Hibernation starts early, in August, and it does not waken before May. In cool weather during the summer it falls into a torpid state. The Northern Birch Mouse has a mixed diet of seeds, berries, and various small animals, especially insects. Pregnancy lasts 4—5 weeks, and a litter usually contains 2—7 young.

The Southern Birch Mouse (*Sicista subtilis*) (2) lives on forested plains from Lake Baikal westward to Bulgaria and Rumania, with isolated populations in Hungary and Austria. Its biology is similar to the Northern Birch Mouse, but it spends less time in hibernation: this begins in September and ends towards the end of April. Birch mice have four cuspidate teeth (3) on either side of their upper jaw, while in the lower jaw there are only three.

The Five-toed Jerboa or Jumping Rat (*Allactaga jaculus*) (4) is a member of the family Dipodidae. In extends from China over central Asia to the Caspian. The Five-toed Jerboa is an inhabitant of steppes and semi-deserts but can also be found in favourable sites in forested plains. It is nocturnal, hiding by day in burrows. There are two types of burrow: permanent ones with usually two entrances and one or more chambers, and simple temporary burrows, mostly with a single entrance, situated only 20—35 cm under the surface. For the winter jerboas dig deep simple burrows, often as much as 2 m deep. They go into hibernation at the onset of the first frosts and waken toward the end of March or beginning of April. Jerboas live on plants but sometimes take insects, such as locusts. The gestation period is 42—45 days, and up to 2 litters of 3—5 young are produced each year.

The Desert Jerboa (*Jaculus jaculus*) (5) is found in north and northeast Africa and in the Near East as far as Iran. It lives in sandy plains, semi-deserts and desert fringes. Its biology is very similar to that of the Five-toed Jerboa. The tunnels it digs may be as much as 3 m long. The nest is usually lined with rootlets and split grass blades.

	Lhb (mm)	Lt (mm)	Lhp (mm)	W (g)
Sicista betulina	50—78	70—105	15—18	5—13
S. subtilis	55—72	67—85	13—17	8—14
Allactaga jaculus	190—250	220—270	85—93	120—200
Jaculus jaculus	120—135	180—195	62—72	60—90

Brown, Common or European Hare

Lepus europaeus

Order: Lagomorpha
Family: Leporidae

The Brown Hare (1) is found throughout most of Europe (with the exception of the Iberian Peninsula) and the Near East. It is native to Britain and has been introduced to northeast Ireland, the Isle of Man and several Scottish islands. It has also been introduced to North and South America, New Zealand and Australia. Originally an inhabitant of plains and open woodland, the hare has become well adapted to cultivated land. It colonizes all sorts of environments and is most common in the lowlands. Although it is solitary, within a given territory a loose group of individuals is formed. In the breeding season hares form larger groups. They are nocturnal, resting all day in shallow depressions (forms) which they dig in sheltered, sunny places (2). Hares feed on grass and leaves, in winter they gnaw the bark of trees and shrubs. The mating season begins as early as January. At this time hares are active even in daytime, several males often pursuing a single female. Gestation lasts 42—44 days. The young, usually 2—4 in number, exceptionally as many as 7, are born covered with fur and with their eyes open (3), and are quite capable of moving around within half an hour of being born. Their mother places them under cover and returns to suckle them, at first two or three times a day but less often after a few days. There may be 3 or 4 litters a year. The female may be fertilized while still pregnant (so-called superfoetation), and thus hares may rapidly increase under favourable conditions.

The range of the African Hare (*Lepus capensis*) (4) includes the southern Iberian Peninsula, Africa, the Near East, and extends across central Asia as far as China. In Asia it is also known as the Tolai. Unlike the Brown Hare, it is more at home in semi-desert and desert regions or in arid, scrubby country. Otherwise there are no differences in the biology of the two species. In some areas it is impossible to distinguish the two types from external features, and they are sometimes amalgamated into a single species — *Lepus capensis*.

In Europe the Mountain, Blue or Arctic Hare (*Lepus timidus*) is found mainly in Scandinavia, from where its range extends throughout the tundra belt all over northern Asia as far as Japan. It was introduced to the Faeroe Islands. In the British Isles it is native in the Scottish Highlands and has been introduced to southern Scotland, northern England, Wales and Ireland. It also occurs in North America. In central Europe it has survived as a relic in the Alps. Except in Ireland where the Mountain Hare keeps its brown coat all the year round, the brown coat is replaced by a white one in winter (5). Mountain Hares are sociable and often live in large colonies. Sometimes they dig short, shallow burrows, and also use shallow depressions in vegetation. The breeding season begins in February and March. Gestation takes 42—45 days, and there are 2 or 3 litters a year. A litter usually includes 2—5 young, litters of 12 young have been reported. The young are suckled more frequently than in the Brown Hare and start taking solid food at around 1 week.

	Lhb (cm)	Lt (cm)	Le (cm)	Lhp (cm)	W (kg)
Lepus europaeus	50—70	7—11	12—14	12—15	2.5—7
L. capensis	40—45	8—10	8—11	9—12	1.5—2.5
L. timidus	52—65	4.5—7	6—9.5	12—16	2—6

Rabbit
Oryctolagus cuniculus

Order: Lagomorpha
Family: Leporidae

The Rabbit's (1) original home was the western Mediterranean, the Iberian Peninsula and northwestern Africa. But natural spread and its introduction by man have made it common in most of Europe, and it has even been imported to other continents. In Australia, for example, Rabbit populations increased enormously and caused great damage. It is not found in Italy, most of the Balkan Peninsula and Scandinavia. It has also been introduced to some parts of the former USSR. The Rabbit was introduced to the British Isles by the Normans in the 12th century. It is most abundant in the west; in the 19th century it spread to the Scottish Highlands, and in the 20th century to Ireland. The Rabbit likes dry sites with light soil in which it can dig its burrows. It is also found in open woodland, and in large city parks. Rabbit colonies (warrens) are sometimes very large. Rabbits excavate residential burrows interconnected by a network of tunnels (2) and pathways, simple, short burrows serving as a temporary shelter (3), and simple nesting burrows where the young are born and tended. If the female leaves a nest with small young, she seals the entrance with a thick plug of clay and grass (4). The ground around the warren is often quite bare and marked with characteristic small, round droppings. Rabbits also mark the boundaries of their territory by the scent from chin glands (5). They usually come out at twilight and at night. They are extremely wary and signal danger by thumping on the ground with their hindfeet, whereupon all rabbits nearby withdraw to the burrows or to dense undergrowth. The female may produce as many as 5 litters (3–8 in a litter) a year. After a pregnancy of 30 days the young are born in a nest lined with dry grass and fur stripped from the female's underparts. Newborn young are naked and blind (6), and their eyes open at about 10 days. The female nurses them for about 3 weeks, after which they can manage alone but continue to live in the colony. They mature at the age of 5—8 months. Rabbits have been bred for meat and for their fur for centuries. They are also popular pets and are used as laboratory animals.

The Gundi (*Ctenodactylus gundi*) (7) is a rodent of the family Ctenodactylidae, living in rocky regions in northeastern Africa. It is diurnal, and its feet are protected from sun-baked rocks by a lining of tough bristles on the soles. The Gundi feeds on desert plants, and apparently never drinks, although it may lick the dew that forms on the rocks. It lives in small colonies and little is known about its reproduction. Mating occurs in January and again in April, the female giving birth to 2—3 young after a pregnancy of 60—70 days.

	Lhb (cm)	Lt (mm)	Lhp (mm)	W (kg)
Oryctolagus cuniculus	38—55	45—70	75—95	1.3—2.5
Ctenodactylus gundi	18—25	25—35	25—30	0.17—0.195

Wild Boar
Sus scrofa

Order: Artiodactyla
Family: Suidae

The Wild Boar (1) is widespread over most of continental Europe and in Asia, and is found also on Sumatra and Java and in north Africa. It has been introduced in places to North and South America. It used to be common in the British Isles but was wiped out by the beginning of the 17th century. Its distribution is discontinuous as it is a typical forest-dweller preferring damp deciduous woodland. It can also be found in wetlands and in the maquis of North Africa. High mountains and continuous areas of cultivation are avoided. Females and juveniles form herds, while old males live in seclusion and half-grown males usually form separate male herds. By day Wild Boars usually take cover in thickets, coming out after dusk in quest of food. They are omnivorous, particularly liking acorns, beechnuts, the swollen underground stems of bracken, willow-herb, cow-parsnip, goutworts, plantain, and various grasses. They also eat insects and grubs, voles, bird's eggs and nestlings, and often will take carrion. They pick the food from the surface of the ground, or root for it with the snout which is strengthened by a cartilaginous plate at the end and a flat bone inside. The rutting season starts in November and lasts until January. At this time of the year the males' flanks develop a layer of ligaments under the skin which affords protection in fights against rivals. Fighting males try to inflict wounds with their sharp 'tusks', which are long canines in the lower and upper jaw (2). In the rutting season males join the herds and each male rounds up a harem of several females which he guards. Gestation takes 114-140 days, the duration depending on the female's age on one hand, and the size of the litter on the other. A litter can contain 3—12 young. Before delivery the female gathers leaves and twigs (4) with which she builds a nest. The young are very delicate as they cannot yet regulate their body temperature efficiently. They stay in the nest for about a week before setting out to follow their mother. Piglets are rusty-coloured, with pale longitudinal stripes (1). They are suckled by the female for about 2 months (3). Young females quickly attain maturity and often mate in their first year of life. Males mature later, sometimes not until 3—4 years old.

The Wild Boar is the remote ancestor of the domestic pig. Domestication took place around the 9th or 8th millennium B.C. in three separate areas: southeastern Asia, around the Mediterranean, and in northeastern Europe. Of all domestic animals the pig can most easily revert to the wild. Escapees can interbreed with the Wild Boar, and, with time, their descendants can hardly be told apart. Such pigs are found especially in some parts of southeastern Asia. In the tracks of the Wild Boar the prints of dew claws on either side overlap those of the cleaves in width (5). Droppings are easily recognizable, being made up of smaller pieces (6).

	Lhb (cm)	Lt (cm)	H (cm)	W (kg)
Sus scrofa	120—200	20—40	80—115	50—250

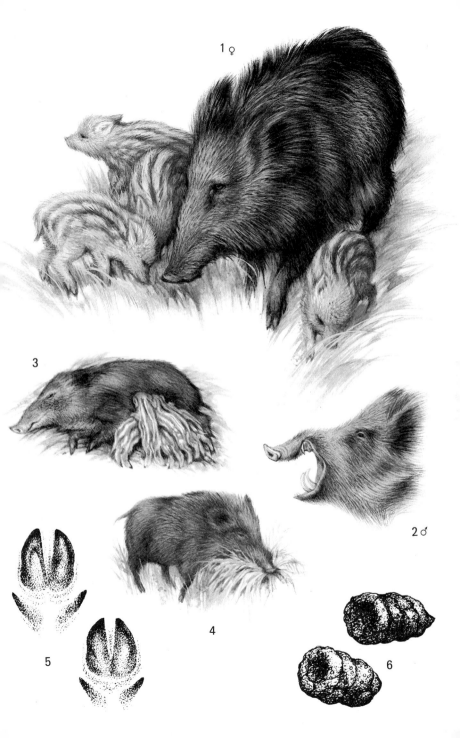

1 ♀

3

2 ♂

5

4

6

Elk or **Moose**
Alces alces

Order: Artiodactyla
Family: Cervidae

The Elk (1) is an inhabitant of the forests of the northern hemisphere. It prefers damp deciduous forests containing alders, poplars, birches and willows. It can often be found at the waterside grazing on submerged plants. Elks are mostly solitary. Even in the mating season, which begins in September, it is usual to find a male in company with a single female only. If three or four Elks are seen together at this time of year, they are almost certainly a female with her young born in the present and in the preceding year. When two males in rut meet, they fight violently. In May or at the beginning of June, after a pregnancy of 225—240 days, the female gives birth to either one or two calves, rusty-brown in colour and about 78—80 cm tall (2). Their mortality is high: approximately a quarter, in some years almost a half, of the calves die in their first year. Those that survive develop very rapidly. At 6 months the Elk may weigh as much as 130 kg, at 1¹/₂ years it has usually reached 250 kg, and is sexually mature. Average life-span is 15—16 years, occasionally up to 25 years. Today the Elk is the largest European wild animal. Males bear spade-shaped antlers (1, 4), which are amongst the most powerful in the entire deer family. Some individuals, however, have thinner antlers which do not broaden out at the ends (3, 5). The span of antlers in a fine specimen may be as much as 2 m.

Since Elks are easy to tame, they have been domesticated for centuries. Elks were used as beasts of burden, as riding animals and to draw sledges. Since 1938 domestication on a large scale has been studied in Russia. At Serpuchovsk, near Moscow, young Elks are halter-broken, tethered and lunged at the age of 2 to 3 months. At 6 months they are trained to carry or pull loads, or to carry a rider. This training takes 3 years. Because they are so sure-footed, domesticated Elks may well turn out to be useful to those who hunt and work in the taiga (forests), especially as riding animals and beasts of burden.

In Europe Elks have recently reappeared in places where they were wiped out several decades ago. They arrive along the old migratory routes and, being capable of covering dozens of kilometres during the night, they can appear quite unexpectedly. Elks spreading westward most often come from deer parks in northern Poland. Since they do not avoid people, many animals attempt to resettle the places from where their ancestors were driven out and fall victim to unscrupulous hunters.

	Lhb (cm)	Lt (cm)	H (cm)	W (kg)
Alces alces	220—230	10—12	150—250	250—600

1 ♂

5

3

4

2

Reindeer
Rangifer tarandus

Order: Artiodactyla
Family: Cervidae

Reindeer (1) are the only deer species in which the females also grow antlers, but, as a rule, the females' antlers are weaker and less branched. The Reindeer is a typical inhabitant of the tundra in Europe, Asia and America. In Europe some populations remain at higher elevations in Norway, on Iceland, in eastern Finland, and in the northern European parts of the former USSR. In Britain the Reindeer used to live in the north of Scotland, but was exterminated in the 12th century. In 1952 however, Reindeer from Sweden were introduced to the Cairngorms. The southern limit of its distribution is the start of the northern forests. In the tundra the surface layer of snow and ice melts for only a few months in the year. Since, however, the water does not soak far into the still-frozen ground, extensive swampy areas arise. The feet of Reindeer are excellently adapted to such terrain: the hooves are broad and widely splayed with the dew claws touching the ground and preventing the animal from sinking. Reindeer live in herds, and usually undertake long seasonal migrations, from the forest in winter to the tundra in summer. During the summer they often seek higher ground as the low-lying tundra is infested with swarms of gnats and flies. In the autumn they return to low-lying pastures. During the summer Reindeer feed on grass, dwarf birches and willows, and fungi. In winter they root for lichen with their antlers and hooves and nibble bark. Only exceptionally does the Reindeer eat moss. The rut (2) falls in autumn. In Norway it may begin towards the end of September but usually it takes place in October and November. Each male holds a harem of around 20 females, and males fight against each other. When in rut males cease feeding and often lose several tens of kilograms in weight. After a pregnancy of 192–246 days, Reindeer females regularly give birth to a single young weighing around 4.5–6 kg (3). The mother with her newborn calf keep away from the herd for several days. Soon, however, they rejoin the herd to move over the grazing lands.

Domesticated Reindeer are far more commonly encountered than wild Reindeer. About 2 million domestic Reindeer live in the northern parts of Scandinavia, in the former USSR and (a few) in Scotland. They are bred both for their hides and for meat, they produce milk and are indispensable draught animals. Domestic Reindeer (4) are somewhat smaller than their wild ancestors and much more variable in colour; they may even be speckled. Domestic Reindeer live more or less freely in herds on pastureland. In the rutting season breeders drive them together, each selects his own Reindeer which are marked by ear notches, the young are notched, and males are castrated. Individuals are caught by lassoes thrown over the antlers. One or more Reindeer are used to draw sledges. A Reindeer can pull a sledge carrying a load of 75–150 kg for up to 160 km a day (the usual distance covered is about 30–40 km). In summer Reindeer are usually used as beasts of burden, carrying loads of about 40 kg for 4–5 hours at a time.

	Lhb (cm)	Lt (cm)	H (cm)	W (kg)
Rangifer tarandus	130—220	15—20	100—120	80—150

4

1 ♂

2 ♀   ♂   3

Roe Deer

Order: Artiodactyla

Capreolus capreolus

Family: Cervidae

The Roe Deer is the smallest European deer. The male (buck) bears simple antlers, with no more than three tines on each stem ('beam'). The summer coat (June—September) is reddish-brown (1, 2); the thicker winter coat is grey or greyish-brown. The Roe Deer is widespread over most of Europe and the cooler parts of Asia as far as China. In Britain it occurs in the wild in Scotland, northern England, Dorset, Devon and Sussex, and is also often to be seen in parks. Its natural habitat is open woodland or the edges of forests, it is not found on the tundra or the dry steppes and semi-deserts. Roe Deer live solitarily or in small family groups. In unfavourable conditions when food is scarce larger groups assemble (which may consist of up to 100 individuals). These groups break up in spring when the males start cleaning their antlers. Wherever they live undisturbed, Roe Deer are active even in the daytime. In cultivated countryside, however, they do not emerge before dusk. The Roe Deer's rutting season lasts from mid-July to mid-August. Before copulation the buck (1) chases the doe round in circles. There is a latent period in pregnancy which prolongs gestation to 9 1/2 months. For females that fail to become pregnant during the summer rutting season, a second mating takes place towards the end of November or in December. Pregnancy following this mating has no delayed implantation and lasts only 5 months. Towards the end of May or at the beginning of June, 1—2, rarely 3, young are born, their white-spotted coats affording excellent camouflage. The mother conceals them and only visits them to suckle. At around 2 weeks the young start following their mother (2). The development of antlers in the male is hormonally controlled and is also susceptible to external factors (food supply, health and social position, etc.). In certain developmental disorders (for example testicular abnormalities), a formation known as the 'wig' develops on the buck's head (3). Roe Deer tracks are elliptical to ovate, with scarcely discernible pads; the cleaves of the forefoot (4) are larger than those of the hindfoot (5). Dew claws are rarely outlined.

Two deer species native to China have been successfully introduced to some parts of England and France: the Chinese or Reeve's Muntjac (*Muntiacus reevesi*) (6) and the Chinese Water Deer (*Hydropotes inermis*) (7). The Muntjac was introduced to the park-like countryside of southern and central England in 1900. It is either solitary or forms small groups and is mostly active at night. In England the rutting season is at the beginning of the year, and one or two white-spotted young are born after a gestation of 6—6 1/2 months. The Chinese Water Deer originally comes from the eastern Yang-tse basin. It was introduced to several deer parks in southern England from where it has spread throughout southeastern England and formed feral populations. The Chinese Water Deer is nocturnal and solitary. In England it mates from November to January. At this time males emit chirping sounds and inflict deep wounds on each other with the long upper canines. Neither sex bears antlers. Twins or triplets are born after a pregnancy of about 6 1/2 months. Occasionally, however, the female may produce as many as 6—7 fawns.

	Lhb (cm)	Lt (mm)	H (cm)	W (kg)
Capreolus capreolus	90—135	25—35	70—90	18—30
Muntiacus reevesi	80—90	100—130	37—50	14—22
Hydropotes inermis	75—100	50—80	45—60	12—16

Fallow Deer
Dama dama

Order: Artiodactyla
Family: Cervidae

The Fallow Deer (1) comes originally from southern Europe and Asia Minor. It has been introduced to other parts of Europe for centuries however. It was introduced into Britain by the Phoenicians or the Romans and now is relatively common in English woodlands, but rarer in the rest of the British Isles. Its range is discontinuous and in many parts of Europe it may only be seen in parks. Here Fallow Deer developed many colour variations ranging from white to black (2).

In summer the Fallow Deer wears a reddish-brown coat with pale spots on the back (1), in winter the coat becomes greyish-brown and the spot pattern is less conspicuous, or entirely absent (3). The rump is fringed with black and, together with the tail which has a prominent black line, is important in communication. The antlers of the adult male (1) are flattened and palmate. Fallow Deer typically live in lowland deciduous and mixed woodland. They live in herds, with females and young usually separated from the males. Their diet is mainly grass and herbage; in the autumn Fallow Deer feed on acorns and beechnuts, and in winter they often nibble the bark of trees. In the rut which lasts from mid-October to November, the bucks gather a greater number of does and emit grunting sounds. Fights between bucks are common, the rivals running against each other with bent heads, butting each other with their antlers. The gestation period is 7 1/2 months. At the beginning of June the female gives birth to one, sometimes two, spotted fawns which are suckled for 6—9 months. Fallow Deer reach sexual maturity as late as their third year.

The White-tailed or Virginian Deer (*Odocoileus virginianus*) is widespread in North and Central America and has been introduced into the wild in Finland, the Czech Republic and Slovakia. It is also to be seen in deer parks on the Continent. White-tailed Deer often live in small groups or solitarily, in winter they sometimes form larger herds. They are diurnal but if they suffer any interference they become extremely shy. When disturbed they display the white underside of the tail as an alarm signal (4), which causes the whole herd to take flight. Their diet consists mostly of leaves and the shoots of shrubs and trees, in spring they feed on the new grass and sprouting corn. In summer they eat various fruits, and in autumn acorns, beechnuts and other nuts. In winter they bite off twigs and dig for roots. The rut takes place in October and the beginning of November. Males in rut emit hissing sounds. Outside the rut the White-tailed Deer is rarely heard, and then mostly at night. Pregnancy lasts around 6 1/2–7 weeks. Females usually give birth to twins which, as in most other deer species, are spotted. The young are only suckled for 2 months. At about 3 weeks the fawns follow their mother and take solid food. They mature when less than 2 years old. The White-tailed Deer is relatively shortlived. Even in its native home the average life span is only 10 years.

	Lhb (cm)	Lt (cm)	H (cm)	W (kg)
Dama dama	130—150	16—30	80—110	30—100
Odocoileus virginianus	180—190	15—30	90—105	30—120

4

1 ♂

3

2

Red Deer
Cervus elaphus

Order: Artiodactyla
Family: Cervidae

The Red Deer (1) is widespread throughout the whole of Europe, from the British Isles eastwards, and throughout northern Asia to the Far East. It is also found in North America where it is known as the Wapiti. In northwestern Africa it has been wiped out in most areas, except in Tunisia. Fairly recently Red Deer from Spain were introduced into Morocco and have successfully adapted. Red Deer have also been introduced into Australia, New Zealand and Argentina. In the British Isles it is found in Scotland, some areas of Ireland and in England, especially Devon, Somerset, and the Lake District. Its true home is woodland, in some areas it also inhabits riverside forests and wetlands. For most of the year the sexes live in separate groups. Females form larger herds, males either live solitarily or in small groups of several younger males. Throughout the day they stay concealed in dense undergrowth and do not come out to feed until dusk. They eat various grasses, the foliage and shoots of shrubs and trees, and in winter they like to strip the bark from trees. Feeding damage left behind by Red Deer is of a typical form (2). Red Deer like wallowing in swampy ground. Besides helping the animal groom its coat and keep cool, wallowing has a major role in the Red Deer's social life. The order in which individuals wallow strengthens the social structure of the group. The rut starts in September and ends at the beginning of October. At this time, the stags' loud roaring can be heard, and there is much fighting between rival stags. When in rut, stags regularly cease to eat, spending their time rounding up a group of hinds and guarding them against other stags. This social structure prevails until winter when the herds break up. Gestation lasts 8 months. The hind usually gives birth to a single calf, rarely two. These are spotted and remain hidden in the first days after birth. They are suckled for approximately 6 months, and usually attain sexual maturity in their third year. As young males are frequently driven away not only by older stags but also by the hinds, mating is postponed until later on.

The Sika Deer (*Cervus nippon*) (3, summer coat; 4, winter coat) is an inhabitant of eastern Asia. It has been introduced to several places in Europe, the United States and New Zealand. In 1860 it was brought to the British Isles and may now be found in England, Scotland and Ireland. The Sika Deer is highly adaptable and lives in deciduous or coniferous forests. It forms small herds, old males preferring to live on their own. The rut starts towards the end of October or in November, when the stags' penetrating whistle may be heard. Each stag herds together three or four hinds. After a pregnancy of about 8 months, a single spotted calf is born. The Sika Deer can interbreed with the Red Deer, which is undesirable as it may endanger the integrity of the Red Deer as a species.

	Lhb (cm)	Lt (cm)	H (cm)	W (kg)
Cervus elaphus	170—260	12—15	120—150	70—250
Cervus nippon	100—155	17—27	75—110	17—120

2

1 ♂   ♀

4 ♂

3 ♂

Saiga
Saiga tatarica

Order: Artiodactyla
Family: Bovidae

From the end of the Ice Ages up to the 17th century, the steppes of eastern Europe and Asia were crowded with Saiga — an antelope related to gazelle. Even in the 19th century, travellers referred to an 'incredible abundance' of Saiga studding the steppes stretching from the Volga to the Urals. Yet man rapidly contributed to their near extinction. Saigas were hunted with borzois and trained eagles, and in winter they were driven onto the ice and clubbed to death. Whole herds were cruelly done to death by being chased into nets or onto the ends of sharp stakes. In the winter of 1828—29 the Saiga became extinct between the Volga and the Urals, and towards the end of World War I, when the number of Saiga fell to less than 1,000 individuals, the species seemed to be approaching complete extinction. Rescue came at the last moment. Hunting was strictly prohibited by law and in the 1920s and 1930s, their numbers started to increase and today may again be counted in millions. Saigas live on most of the steppe plants. Their lungs are protected against the frequent duststorms by a long curved muzzle which acts as a filter (3). The mucous membranes in the muzzle also help to warm the air breathed in during winter blizzards. The rut begins in early November. The males (1, winter coat) put on weight, their muzzle swells and a dark liquid exudes from glands beneath the eyes. Each ram herds together a large number of hornless ewes (2) over which he keeps guard. When in rut rams cease feeding and markedly lose weight; weakened animals often die towards the end of the winter. Their place is then taken by young males who have not yet taken part in the rut. In April or at the beginning of May, after a gestation of 5—5^1/$_2$ months, the ewe gives birth to her young — usually twins. The ewe then conceals the lambs in the steppe and revisits them for brief intervals for suckling. Often suckling takes no more than a few seconds. Like most animals of the open plains Saigas move with an ambling gait. They start to run by taking several leaps which turn into a gallop.

The Dorcas Gazelle (*Gazella dorcas*) (5) is found throughout north Africa, over the Sinai Peninsula to the Near East. It is an inhabitant of semi-deserts and deserts, usually forming small groups of 3—20 individuals. The Dorcas Gazelle is threatened by overhunting and has already been exterminated in many parts of its original range.

The Slender-horned Gazelle (*Gazella leptoceros*) (4) is discontinuously distributed over sandy areas to the north of the Sahara. It is extremely shy. According to the IUCN (International Union for the Conservation of Nature), its complete extermination is sadly only a matter of a few years. Gazelles breed throughout the year. Gestation takes 5—6 months in the Dorcas Gazelle, 6—7 months in the Slender-horned Gazelle. Both species produce a single young, which is suckled for around 4—6 months.

	Lhb (cm)	Lt (cm)	H (cm)	W (kg)
Saiga tatarica	120—135	8—12	60—80	23—40
Gazella dorcas	80—100	12—15	53—61	12—16
G. leptoceros	90—110	14—16	60—66	14—17

1 ♂

3

4 ♂

5 ♂

2 ♀

Chamois
Rupicapra rupicapra

Order: Artiodactyla
Family: Bovidae

The Chamois (1) lives in the high mountains of southern and central Europe. Its range ends in the north in the Tatras Mountains in Slovakia and in the east in the Caucasus. It can also be found in the Near East. In the higher mountains it lives on the open rocky slopes above the forest belt, coming down to shelter in the trees in winter. In lower mountain ranges it prefers the upper edge of the forests. Chamois live in herds. Females and young form larger herds, each guided by an old female. Younger males associate into less numerous 'stag herds', old males prefer to live solitarily. In the rut males join the herds of females. In summer chamois graze in alpine meadows and eat the leaves and shoots of mountain shrubs and trees; in winter they feed on dry grass and lichens, gnaw bark and even eat conifer needles. Chamois are diurnal and only rarely can be seen moving about on moonlit nights. The rut begins in November and December, or even in October in particularly cold weather. In warmer weather the rut lasts shorter or may not happen at all. Males in rut often make bleating noises. The herds become restless as the males pursue rivals, take up threatening postures (3) and fight. At this time they also mark their home range with the secretion of scent glands located behind the horns (2). After a pregnancy of 6—6$^{1}/_{2}$ weeks the female gives birth to a single young, usually in an inaccessible place among the rocks. Two hours after birth the young can already follow its mother. For about 6 weeks more the mother and young stay away from the herd. The young is suckled for about 6 months, and reaches sexual maturity at 2$^{1}/_{2}$ to 3 years.

The Chamois is excellently adapted for moving over difficult, rocky terrain. The rims of the cleaves of its hooves are sharp edged, preventing it from slipping and enabling it to get a footing even in small holds in the rock face. The cleave prints of Chamois are wedge-shaped and separated by a wide gap (4). A slow, easy walk leaves no imprint of dew claws (5), whereas when running and jumping the hindfeet are placed in front of the forefeet and imprints of dew claws become clearly outlined (6) as the legs bend. Chamois characteristically frisk and play even when alone, and especially when they come upon snow in the summertime, or when they set foot upon mossy ground. They run in circles or figures-of-eight, making occasional leaps, rearing and kicking their heels in the air. Sometimes, apparently simply for fun, Chamois will climb up steep snow-slopes and slide down again on their rump with forelegs outstretched.

In all the European mountain ranges Chamois are now endangered by the impact of man, by tourism and winter sports.

	Lhb (cm)	Lt (cm)	H (cm)	W (kg)
Rupicapra rupicapra	90—140	3—8	70—100	12—40

Wild Goat

Capra aegagrus

Order: Artiodactyla
Family: Bovidae

The original natural range of the Wild Goat extends from the eastern Mediterranean, including some of the islands, over the Near East to central Asia. In many parts of its original range it is now extinct, elsewhere Domestic Goats have been introduced and have interbred, diluting the original Wild Goat population. True Wild Goats may be found, for example, on Crete in the Lefka-Ori Mountains, and on the tiny island of Erimomilos. Elsewhere in Europe 'wild' goats will be descendants of escaped Domestic Goats. The Wild Goat is a typical inhabitant of rocky terrain. It lives in small herds, males (1) and females (2) forming separate groups. Old males prefer to live solitarily. At rest the herd stays in one place but individuals keep their distance from each other. Only the young lie in close physical contact with their mother. Goats graze from dawn until mid-morning, then lie down to rest and resume feeding in the afternoon. They will eat any kind of vegetation and since ancient times have contributed to the bare open country of much of the Mediterranean. In the Mediterranean region mating takes place in October, further east in November and December. Pregnancy lasts 5 months, and before delivery the females leave the herd to search for the most inaccessible places. Here they give birth to 1 or 2 young. For the first few days the young stay concealed among the rocks. After 3—4 days they start to follow the mother and soon accompany her, climbing nimbly over the rocks. The mother then returns to the herd with her young, which are suckled for about six months. The young stay with their mother until she gives birth again; if she does not become pregnant, they will continue to live with her. Both sexes carry sabre-shaped, backward-curving horns, which in males are longer and also flattened from the side to form a sharp front edge, crossed with thickened ridges (3). In the cross-section the horn is drop-shaped with a rounded front surface. In the Domestic Goat (*Capra hircus*) the back edge is not so sharp, the ridges are finer, and the inner side of the horn is flat or only slightly convex (4). The Wild Goat is the ancestor of the Domestic Goat. Domestication occurred around the seventh millennium B.C., making goats an older domestic animal than, for example, cattle. The older breeds of Domestic Goats (and even some very new ones) possess sabre-shaped horns like those of the Wild Goat. More commonly, however, the horns of Domestic Goats curve in a slight spiral away from the body. This may be due to a mutation or to other species of wild goats in their ancestry.

	Lhb (cm)	Lt (cm)	H (cm)	W (kg)
Capra aegagrus	120—160	15—20	70—100	25—40

1 ♂

4

3

2

Ibex
Capra ibex

Order: Artiodactyla
Family: Bovidae

The natural home of the Ibex is above the timberline in the Swiss, Italian, French, Austrian and Bavarian Alps. As early as the 16th century, however, it was threatened with extinction by overhunting, and in spite of strict prohibitions on hunting numbers dwindled so rapidly that, in 1816, almost the last 50 Ibexes in Europe remained in the Piedmontese Gran Paradiso. These were saved by the energetic intervention of King Victor Emmanuel II. Another small group of Ibexes survived around Salzburg. Since then the Ibex has been strictly protected, has multiplied and been reintroduced to some of its previous localities. Outside its natural range it has been introduced into Yugoslavia. Ibexes live above the tree line, only in April and May descending to the upper forest belt. From spring to autumn, males (1) and females live in separate herds. In the rut, in December and January, males join the female herds. Males frequently fight even before the rut; however, these are usually purely ritual combats doing no harm to the animals involved (2). Towards the end of May or the beginning of June, a single young is born after a gestation of 5—6 months. For the first few hours after birth the mother keeps a watchful eye on her young but soon the young follows its mother wherever she goes. Females remain in the herd but males leave the herd at 2—4 years to join a 'stag group'. Both sexes have horns; in males, however, they are far more powerful, up to 1 m long, with large projections on the thickened front part.

Other European mountain ranges have their own Ibex species which do not occur anywhere else (endemic species). The Pyrenean Ibex (*Capra pyrenaica*) (3) lives in the Pyrenees; the Caucasian Ibex (*Capra caucasica*) (4) in the western Caucasus; the Daghestan Ibex (*Capra cylindricornis*) (5) in the eastern Caucasus. Individual species show differences not only in colouring but also in the shape and size of their horns and in some details of their way of life. Like the Alpine Ibex, all these other Ibex species are in danger of extinction and are included in the IUCN 'Red List'. Most endangered is the Pyrenean Ibex which has already been completely exterminated in many places. In the Caucasus numbers appear also to be falling. All individuals living in captivity have been registered and a breeding book has been established which is kept at the Schönbrunn Zoological Garden in Vienna.

	Lhb (cm)	Lt (cm)	H (cm)	W (kg)
Capra ibex	115—170	10—20	65—105	35—150
C. pyrenaica	100—140	10—15	65—70	35—80
C. caucasica	130—155	10—18	80—100	50—70
C. cylindricornis	130—160	10—15	80—100	34—100

1 ♂

3 ♂

4 ♂

5 ♂

2

Mouflon
Ovis orientalis

Order: Artiodactyla
Family: Bovidae

In the late Stone Age the Mouflon, the ancestor of the domestic sheep, was still common in the forested plains and mountains of south central Europe to the Mediterranean. Today its natural range is restricted to the Mediterranean region and the Near East. In the western part of this range, on Corsica, about 100 Mouflons can be seen in the Asco Reserve in the Mont-Cinto Mountains and in the deer park of Baella in the Solenzara Mountains. In eastern Sardinia, also, approximately 400 individuals live in the regions of Monti del Gennargentu, Supramonte di Orgosolos and Monte Albo. Two populations were reintroduced to the islands of Asinara and Capo Figari lying to the north of Sardinia. Animals in this western population are sometimes given the scientific name of *Ovis musimon* but they are now thought not to be specifically distinct from the race which occurs further east.

In the eastern Mediterranean and the Near East, the species is represented by a distinctive race, sometimes called the Red Sheep (6), whose westernmost locality is on Cyprus. The Mouflon's original habitat in the Mediterranean is the maquis and high grassy pastures and the edges of deciduous forests and pine groves. Since the 18th century Mouflons of the western race have been introduced to reserves and hunting grounds all over Europe, and today many thousands may be found in all European countries. They have also been introduced to America, to Hawaii and the Kerguelen Islands. The Mouflon eats grass and leafy twigs, especially of the Strawberry Tree (*Arbutus*) and Broom (*Cytisus*). From spring to autumn males and females live in separate groups. In the mating period, which begins in October and ends in December, males join the herds of females and lambs without, however, taking a leading role. The herd remains under the leadership of an old ewe. Males sometimes fight against each other. As a rule, however, the rut is relatively peaceful. After a pregnancy of five months the female gives birth to one, sometimes two young which develop rapidly.

Mouflon males (1) have powerful, notched, sickle-shaped horns up to 90 cm long. Their length, strength and degree of curl correspond to the animal's age. Females either grow only small short horns or, more often, they are hornless (2). The Mouflon is well equipped for moving on stony ground. Its legs are relatively short and strong, the front part of the cleaves of the hoofs is slender and pointed, and the edges are sharp. Cleave prints are ovate or elliptical in outline, the tips are widely spread. A sharp ridge is easily discernible on the edge of the track; the outer tips of both fore and hind cleaves point inwards. When walking the Mouflon places its hindfeet in the tracks of its forefeet (3), when running the hindfeet are placed in front of the forefeet. Dew-claw prints are visible only in very soft ground (4).

The mountainous regions of the North African desert are the home of the Barbary Sheep or Aoudad (*Ammotragus lervia*) (5). At present its numbers are dwindling rapidly due to overhunting. Barbary Sheep live in groups, old males live solitarily. They rest throughout the day and emerge to graze at night. In the short growth period they graze grass and herbage, for the rest of the year they have to survive on dry grass, lichens and twigs. Mating takes place in November. After a pregnancy of 5—5^1/$_2$ months females give birth to one, or very often two, young.

	Lhb (cm)	Lt (cm)	H (cm)	W (kg)
Ovis musimon	80—125	7—15	60—90	20—60
O. orientalis	130—150	7—15	80—95	35—90
Ammotragus lervia	130—165	15—25	75—100	40—130

1 ♂

3

4

2 ♀

5

6

Wisent or European Bison
Bison bonasus

Order: Artiodactyla
Family: Bovidae

The Wisent (1) once used to inhabit woodland throughout Europe, reaching east-wards as far as the Caucasus. But as the forests disappeared and the landscape was transformed the Wisent was increasingly forced out into inaccessible places and slowly disappeared from Europe. By the Middle Ages it was extinct in most of Europe, and survived only in the virgin forests of eastern Europe and in the Cauca-sus. The Caucasian Wisent constituted an independent subspecies, *Bison bonasus caucasicus* (3); eastern European Wisents belong to the subspecies *Bison bona-sus bonasus* (2). At the beginning of the last century, a population of around 300—500 lived in the Bialowieza virgin forest on the Polish-Russian border. In World War I, after the front had swept over this area, numbers were considerably reduced. Wisents also suffered greatly from poaching. The last Wisent living in the wild was shot on 9 February 1921, by the forester Bartolomeus Szpakowicz. However, there were still 56 Wisents living in zoos and private parks, which are the ancestors of all present-day individuals. The International Association for the Survival of Wisents took charge of their rescue, a stud book was established, the numbers in captivity started to increase and in 1956, Wisents were reintroduced to the Bialowieza forest. The history of the Caucasian Wisent is far sadder: all efforts to save it have failed. In the 18th and the 19th centuries, Wisents still occurred in relative abundance in the northwestern Caucasus. Towards the end of the 19th century, however, their numbers were rapidly decreasing. In the 1880s approxi-mately 800—1,000 individuals were estimated, in the 1890s only 400—700. In 1920 no more than 100 Wisents could be found in the Caucasus, and a year later their numbers had decreased to a half. In 1924 a preserve was established but the Cau-casian Wisent could not be saved, the last dying in 1927.

Wisents live in herds led by an adult bull. Old bulls prefer to live alone. Wisents set out to graze early in the morning and at night. They feed on anything they can find in the rich forest undergrowth, especially on the foliage and shoots of various shrubs and trees, more rarely on grass. Mating begins in August and the season may be protracted until October. Cows give birth to a single young (4) after a pregnancy of 9 months. Its development is slow. Sexual maturity is not reached until 7—8 years, and physical development is not completed until about 10 years.

In some parts of southern Europe (e.g. Bulgaria, Albania, Italy, Hungary and Ru-mania), the Near East, and in north Africa (mainly in Egypt) we may come across the Water Buffalo or Carabao (*Bubalus arnee* f. *bubalis*) (5). This is a domesticat-ed form of the Indian Buffalo (*Bubalus arnee*) indigenous to India. The Water Buf-falo is an important domestic animal of the Asian tropics and subtropics, and was brought to Europe by the Turks in the Middle Ages. It has been and still is used for all kinds of work in the fields, and is a good milk-producer. In Italy, buffalo cows yield almost 2,000 litres of milk in one lactation period. The fat content is almost four per cent higher than that of the milk of domestic cattle, and the protein con-tent is higher by one per cent. Pregnancy in buffalo cows is longer than that of cattle, varying between 9 and 9$^{1}/_{2}$ months.

	Lhb (cm)	Lt (cm)	H (cm)	W (kg)
Bison bonasus	300—350	50—60	158—195	450—1,000
Bubalus arnee f. *bubalis*	250—300	60—100	150—180	450—800

1 ♂

4 ♀

5

3

2

Musk-ox
Ovibos moschatus

Order: Artiodactyla
Family: Bovidae

The Arctic tundra, exposed to biting winds, is the home of the Musk-ox (1). Its powerful stature brings to mind wild cattle, but many morphological and anatomical features as well as biochemical evidence relate it to sheep and goats. The coat of the Musk-ox is probably the longest found in mammals. On the back it is 16 cm long but on the neck, chest and rump it may reach a length of 60 cm, often as much as 90 cm. This long thick coat provides the Musk-ox with excellent protection against the severe Arctic cold.

In the Ice Ages Musk-oxen also lived in Europe. As the climate changed, they receded northwards, together with glaciers. Today Musk-oxen can be found in Greenland, on Canadian islands in the Arctic and in several places on the North American coast between the Mackenzie River and Hudson Bay. Musk-oxen have been threatened by overhunting, and in Canada Musk-ox hunting was completely forbidden as early as 1917. Denmark and Norway imposed strict limitations on Musk-ox hunting in 1950. Most attemps to introduce the Musk-ox outside its present range have failed, but animals taken to Spitzbergen and the Dovre mountain range in Norway have survived and reproduced. In all these cases, the subspecies *Ovibos moschatus wardi* (3), native to Greenland, was selected. This has characteristic white hair covering the forehead and the upper part of the head.

Musk-oxen live in herds led by an adult bull. He is accompanied by 2—4 females, the rest of the herd numbering 8, but sometimes as many as 20, juveniles and calves. Old bulls — once leaders of the herd but overcome in violent fights during the rut and driven away by stronger rivals — live in seclusion. Fighting takes place from June to August. The bulls are armed with heavy horns which join across the forehead to form a heavy 'shield'. They run up against each other like rams, clashing their heads together. Their diet depends on the season. In the short Arctic summer, lasting no more than 3 months (from the end of May until the end of August), they eat twigs and leaves of dwarf willows, saxifrages, various grasses and sedges. In winter they take any plant food they can find, mosses and lichens as well as grass. Pregnancy lasts $8^1/_2$ months. Most calves are born towards the end of April or at the beginning of May. Cold weather does not bother them but they are sensitive to wet conditions, and many calves perish when the thaw sets in. Musk-oxen have only one enemy beside man — the Wolf. Wolves have little chance of overcoming an adult Musk-ox, but pursue the calves. When attacked by Wolves, the herd of Musk-oxen forms a circle enclosing the young, while the outer circle is formed by a wall of horns and the frontal shields of adult animals (2). Old bulls make short, violent attacks against the Wolves from whose teeth they are protected by their long, thick coat.

	Lhb (cm)	Lt (cm)	Lhp (cm)	W (kg)
Ovibos moschatus	180—250	7—10	100—145	200—400

Fin Whale or Common Rorqual

Balaenoptera physalus

Order: Cetacea
Family: Balaenopteridae

The Fin Whale (1) occurs world-wide. In the Atlantic Ocean it is most commonly found near Iceland, off the Faeroe Islands and the Norwegian coast, but also appears around Britain and Ireland, mostly from July to September. It is regularly encountered in the western Mediterranean, in particular near Corsica. The Fin Whale sometimes forms large schools but it is more usual to come across two or three individuals together. Fin Whales are baleen whales, feeding on tiny crustacea and small fish which are filtered through plates of whalebone (baleen) (5). Some 500—600 kg of food have been found in the stomachs of captured whales. Fin Whales hunt at relatively shallow depths, even just below the surface.They usually dive for 5—8 minutes and then emerge several times in quick succession to breathe. Like all cetaceans, they exhale before diving, the moist air forming a visible 'spout' in the cooler air outside. Spouts may reach 3—9 m high (2). The direction, height and shape of the spout are characteristic of different species. When in danger, Fin Whales can dive for as long as 20—30 minutes. They regularly mate in winter when most individuals migrate south to warmer waters, and usually do so under water, rarely on the surface. After a pregnancy of 11—12 months, the female gives birth to a single calf which is 6—6.5 m long and weighs 1.5—1.8 tonnes. Like the young of all cetaceans, it is born tail first. The female suckles the young for 6 months when the calf is around 10—12 m long. Fin Whales reach maturity at the age of about 2—3 years.

The Blue Whale (*Balaenoptera musculus*) (3) also has a worldwide distribution but is much rarer than the Fin Whale, due to overhunting in the past. It is the largest living animal, and also the largest that has ever lived. Near British shores it appears to the west of the Hebrides and off the Shetlands, usually in July or August, in winter migrating to warmer subtropical waters. In the Atlantic the Blue Whale can most frequently be found in the area between the Cape Verde Islands and Spitzbergen. The Blue Whale is usually seen swimming alone. It dives for as long as 50 minutes, each deep dive followed by repeated surfacings to breathe. When it breathes out, a spout 6—9 m, exceptionally up to 12 m high is produced. The Blue Whale feeds exclusively on planktonic crustacea (the baleen plates are shown in 6), especially the tiny shrimp-like Krill. Stomachs of caught specimens have contained 1.2—1.5 tonnes of food. The Blue Whale can breed all the year round but usually mates in June and July. Gestation lasts 11 months. The newborn calf is 6—9 m long and weighs 2.5—3 tonnes.

The Sei Whale (*Balaenoptera borealis*) (4) lives in the cold waters of the Arctic. It regularly travels south, to the seas off Iceland, Spitzbergen and Norway, and is sometimes seen off northeast Scotland. It is usually seen swimming singly or in twos. Its diet consists of crustacea, cephalopods and small fish which it usually catches just below the surface. It is not unusual to find 100—400 kg of food in its stomach. The Sei Whale dives for only a short period, 2—12 minutes, then coming to the surface usually twice to breathe. The spouts are around 2—5 m high. It mates throughout the year. Gestation lasts about 1 year, the newborn young is 4—5 m long and weighs about 2 tonnes.

	L (m)	W (t)
Balaenoptera physalus	18—25	33—53
B. musculus	24—32	120—190
B. borealis	15—19	16—20

Humpback Whale

Megaptera novaeangliae

Order: Cetacea
Family: Balaenopteridae

The Humpback Whale (1) is a cosmopolitan species migrating long distances between subtropic and polar waters. It was once found along the entire Atlantic seaboard but whaling resulted in a catastrophic decrease in its numbers. Today it is rarely encountered, usually off Iceland or the Azores. The last Humpback in British waters was recorded in 1913. Since 1966 it is protected throughout the world and numbers have increased slightly, at least in the northwestern Atlantic. Humpback Whales particularly like waters close to land. They swim less quickly than Fin, Blue or Sei Whales but often leap completely out of the water (2). The Humpback Whale feeds on crustacea and small fish, its stomach can contain 500—600 kg of food. When hunting it often changes direction. It usually dives for 3—6 minutes at a time, rarely for 30 minutes. It then surfaces several times (3—8) to breathe. Spouts 2—5 m high are produced when it exhales (3). During mating, which is not confined to a particular season, Humpback Whales are extremely active and make singing or siren-like sounds under the water which are audible for a 100 km. Gestation takes about 1 year. The newborn young measures 4—4.5 m.

The Sperm Whale (*Physeter macrocephalus*) (4) belongs to the family Physeteridae: it is a toothed cetacean of the suborder Odontoceti. It is particularly widespread in warmer subtropical and tropical waters, where the females stay all the year round while the males migrate to the polar regions for the summer. They also enter the Mediterranean quite often. Over the years they have frequently been seen close to the shores in the Atlantic off the British Isles, usually in August. Sperm Whales live in groups of a single male and a harem of several females accompanied by young. Young males form 'stag groups'. The Sperm Whale eats chiefly cephalopods and fish (which may be up to 1 m long), less frequently crustacea. However, a shark 3 m long has been found in the stomach of an adult Sperm Whale. When hunting, the Sperm Whale dives to great depths (over 1,000 m), and spends 10—50 minutes underwater. After diving it stays on the surface for a considerable time. The gestation period is variously estimated to be 10—13 months. The newborn young is 3—5.5. m long and weighs about 1 tonne.

The Pygmy Sperm Whale (*Kogia breviceps*) (5) is an uncommon inhabitant of subtropical and tropical waters, and is encountered from time to time off the shores of Portugal, France, Ireland and the Netherlands. In view of its rarity, very little is known about its biology. Pygmy Sperm Whales mostly appear either singly or in twos, the latter probably being either a pair or a female with her young. The diet consists of cephalopods, mainly cuttle-fish, crabs and fish. Mating usually takes places in spring or autumn. Pregnancy lasts 9 months and the newborn young is about 1 m long. Whales propel themselves chiefly by the anal fin (the fluke). Its shape is typical of each species (6, *M. novaeangliae;* 7, *P. macrocephalus.*)

	L (m)	W (t)
Megaptera novaeangliae	12—16	25—33
Physeter macrocephalus	10—20	10—50
Kogia breviceps	2.5—3	0.3—0.5

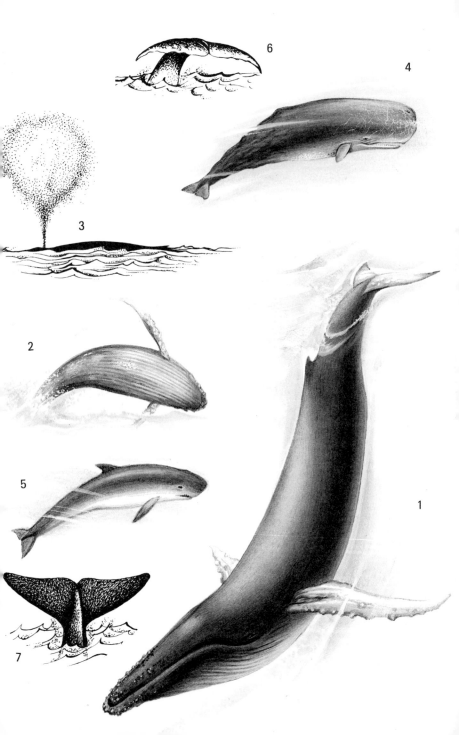

Biscayan or North Atlantic Right Whale
Eubalaena glacialis

Order: Cetacea
Family: Balaenidae

In the past the North Atlantic Right Whale (1) lived throughout the eastern Atlantic between the Bay of Biscay and Spitzbergen, and was even found in the Mediterranean off Italy. In the Middle Ages it was hunted in the English Channel and off the Hebrides until the 18th and the 19th centuries, when numbers rapidly decreased, and in many areas it became extinct. Since 1935 its hunting has been prohibited world-wide. Today the North Atlantic Right Whale is extremely rare in the eastern Atlantic. Once groups of as many as 100 individuals were quite common, now only small groups of 3—4 whales are seen even where it is still relatively common. It is a baleen whale, living on crustacea and molluscs. When hunting the North Atlantic Right Whale dives for 10—20 minutes, yet when in danger it can remain under water for as long as 50 minutes. Each dive is followed by 5 or 6 breaths. Each exhalation is accompanied by a typical double blow (2) to a height of 4—4.5 m. Breeding occurs every other year. After a pregnancy of about 1 year the female usually gives birth to a single young in warm subtropical waters near the coast. The young is 4—5 m long at birth. After being suckled for 6—7 months it grows to about 8.5 m. When young females are about 12 m long, they have already reached sexual maturity and can breed.

The Greenland Right Whale (*Balaena mysticetus*) (3, 4) is an inhabitant of the Arctic. This species was also intensively hunted in the 19th century and its numbers were decimated. Since 1935 its hunting has been prohibited. In the eastern Atlantic it is only seen today around Greenland and Spitzbergen but nevertheless it continues to increase in numbers. The Greenland Right Whale is a solitary animal, only rarely are small groups of 3—5 seen. The Greenland Right Whale feeds on small planktonic crustacea and molluscs, hunting close to the surface and diving usually for 5—10, rarely for 20, minutes. When wounded or pursued, however, whales can remain under water for 40—80 minutes. After diving they come to the surface for around 1—3 minutes during which they exhale (blow) about 4—12 times, producing a double blow reaching 4 m high. The breeding period does not coincide with any particular season but most young are born from February to May. Estimates of gestation time differ from 9.5 to13—14 months. The story that this whale gives birth to her young on an ice-floe is folk-lore, as the evidence suggests that all whales give birth under water. The newborn young of the Greenland Right Whale measures 3—4.5 m.

	L (m)	W (t)
Eubalaena glacialis	13—17	40—50
Balaena mysticetus	15—20	40—55

Beluga or **White Whale**
Delphinapterus leucas

Order: Cetacea
Family: Monodontidae

The Beluga (1) is widespread in the coastal waters of arctic and subarctic regions, right up to the polar ice-sheets. It prefers shallow water and is often found in river estuaries. Thus, for example, a Beluga is spoken of which, in 1966, found its way into the Rhine and proceeded upstream as far as Cologne and Bonn. They are fairly regularly seen off Denmark and Norway, in the North Sea, and off the Scottish coast. They form groups, 'schools', of 5—10, sometimes more than 30. Groups of more than 100 have rarely been encountered. As a rule, females and young form groups separate from the males. The Beluga eats crustacea and fish, particularly cod and, during their seasonal migrations, salmonids. Belugas usually hunt at a depth of approximately 10 m and make dives lasting 3—5, at most 15 minutes. Then they briefly emerge three or four times for air. They also hunt under the ice, and are able to break through 8-cm thick ice in order to breathe. The mating season is usually in April and May. Gestation is estimated at 11—12 months but some experts propose 14—15 months. The female gives birth to a single young, rarely to twins. The newborn young measures 130—150 cm and weighs 60—150 kg, and is greyish-blue (2). After reaching 2.5—3 m long, the young gradually start turning white (3), beginning with the underside of the body. Belugas 4 m long are already pure white.

The Narwhal (*Monodon monoceros*) is a close relative of the Beluga. Its circumpolar distribution covers the Arctic, and it is the most northerly of all cetaceans. It regularly turns up off Spitzbergen, more rarely off the Norwegian coast; stragglers also appear in the North Sea, near the English shores, and it has once been recorded off the Dutch coast. The Narwhal's most conspicuous characteristic, seen only in the male (4) is the forward directed, spirally twisted left incisor of the upper jaw up to 3 m long, forming a tusk. The elongation of both incisors (i.e., the only two teeth the adult Narwhal has) is extremely rare. The shape of the male's anal fin is also quite unique among cetaceans. Narwhals are sociable, living in groups of about 10. They eat mainly cephalopods (e.g., cuttle-fish), less frequently fish and some crustacea. The Narwhal usually remains submerged for 5—10 minutes and then surfaces eight or nine times to breathe in. Breeding is not limited to a particular season but the young are usually born in summer. When in rut, males often come to the surface and cross each other's tusks (6). Sometimes several males may assemble around a single female (5), crossing their tusks above her back. The length of gestation it unknown, but it probably lasts one year. At birth the young are 1.5 m long and weigh 60—80 kg.

	L (m)	W (kg)
Delphinapterus leucas	4—7	800—1,200
Monodon monoceros	4—6	600—1,000

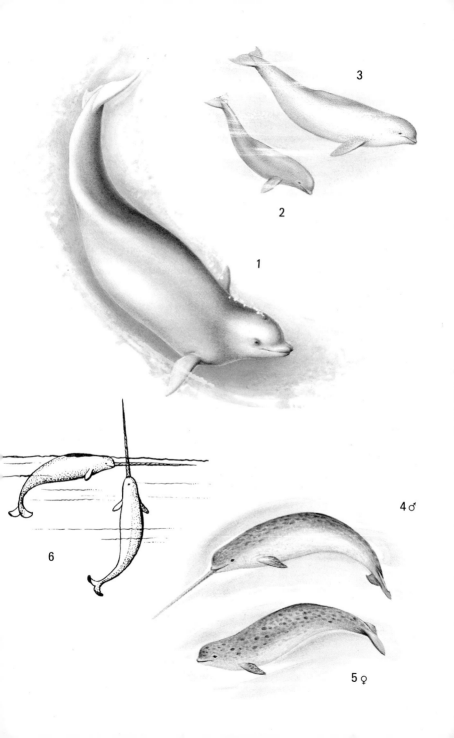

Common Dolphin
Delphinus delphis

Order: Cetacea
Family: Delphinidae

The Common Dolphin (1) is very widespread in the tropical and warm seas throughout the world. It is still fairly common in the Mediterranean as well as in the Black Sea and appears around the British Isles, most frequently in the English Channel and along the coast of Ireland; in the North Sea it is seldom seen. It lives in 'schools', which swim together and also leap above the surface at the same time. It mainly hunts fish, more rarely eating crustacea and molluscs. The dolphin is a rapid swimmer and can travel at a rate of 45—55 km per hour. Dolphins remain submerged for only 0.5—3 minutes, exceptionally for about 5 minutes, and need about 0.2—0.4 seconds to breathe in. The breeding season begins in June and ends in August. At this time 6—8 males cluster round a single female; they chase each other and try to get their teeth into their rivals' fins. Females go through a 10—11 month pregnancy, the newborn young is 80—90 cm long. The young are born tail first in dolphins as well as whales.

The Bottlenosed Dolphin (*Tursiops truncatus*) (2) is found worldwide, and is the commonest species of Europe. Now and then it appears off the southern and western coasts of England and off Ireland. It frequently forms large 'schools' and can remain under water for quite a long time, up to 30 minutes. It mostly feeds on fish and small sharks, less frequently cephalopods and crustacea. The breeding period coincides with the warm months of the year. Pregnancy takes 12 months, the newborn young measures 90—130 cm.

The Common Dolphin and the Bottlenosed Dolphin are the species most commonly kept in dolphinariums, where their ability to learn and their great agility delight visitors. The animals in dolphinariums have been caught in the wild (3).

Risso's Dolphin (*Grampus griseus*) (4) is widely distributed throughout both hemispheres. It occurs from the Mediterranean past the British Isles as far as Scandinavia but does not penetrate beyond the Arctic Circle. It is usually seen in small groups of less than 10 animals, 'schools' comprising more than 100 individuals may occasionally be seen. Risso's Dolphin eats mainly cephalopods (squid etc.). Little is known about its reproduction. The young are usually born in winter, the newborn animal measures 140—160 cm.

The Pilot Whale (*Globicephala melaena*) (5) is an inhabitant of the Atlantic and of the oceans of the southern hemisphere. It is found from the Far North down to the Mediterranean, being most common in the waters around Iceland and to the north of the British Isles, especially near the Orkney and the Shetland Islands. It forms large 'schools' staying close to the surface.

The main component of its diet are cephalopods. Mating takes place in summer. Gestation lasts one year, the newborn young measures 140—200 cm.

	L (m)	W (kg)
Delphinus delphis	1.6—2.9	30—90
Tursiops truncatus	2—3.5	150—200
Grampus griseus	3—4	300—500
Globicephala melaena	6—8	1,500—2,000

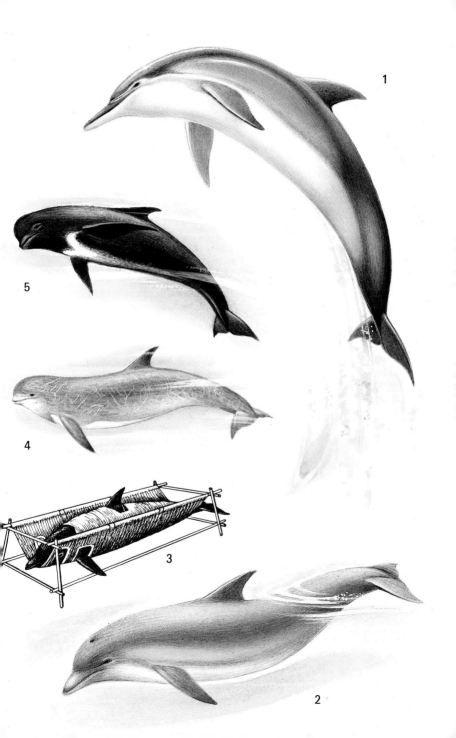

Killer Whale
Orcinus orca

Order: Cetacea
Family: Delphinidae

The range of the Killer Whale (1) stretches from the Arctic to the Antarctic. Although it prefers cold waters, it has been seen all around European seas from the Spitzbergen and Iceland to the Baltic and the Mediterranean. Near the British Isles it is most frequently found off the east coast, rarely off the western or Irish coasts. Killer Whales live in groups of 20—30. Their diet includes not only fish but also marine mammals such as seals and other cetaceans. This seems to vary not only according to the season but also according to the areas in which they are hunting. Sometimes a Killer Whale's stomach is found to contain almost exclusively fish and sharks, sometimes cephalopods predominate, in other cases dolphins or seals. Fourteen seals were found in the stomach of one Killer Whale. In the seals' pupping season Killer Whales often assemble near the seal colonies, lying in wait for easy prey. They also hunt seals by swimming under an ice-floe carrying resting animals, breaking through the ice from below and capturing the seal (2). Whenever a school of Killer Whales comes across a whale, they attack it, tearing flesh from its lips and tongue. Mating may occur at any time of year but most young are born from May to July. Killer Whales have a 16-months' gestation, the newborn young measures 200—275 cm.

The False Killer (*Pseudorca crassidens*) (3) lives in the high seas and very rarely appears near land. Occasionally, however, it appears in coastal waters from Scandinavia to the Mediterranean, and has rarely been seen near the British Isles. It seems that False Killers become disorientated close to the shore and often become stranded. Well-known and often cited is the example of a school of 150 False Killers stranded on the coast of Scotland in 1927. The diet of the False Killer consists of fish and cephalopods. The gestation period is approximately 14 months, the newborn young is 160—180 cm long.

The Common Porpoise (*Phocaena phocaena*) (4) inhabits coastal waters from the White Sea through the North Sea to the Baltic and down the Atlantic seaboard to the Mediterranean and the Black Sea. In the Mediterranean it appears rarely, whereas in the Black Sea it occurs in large numbers. Near the British Isles it is chiefly seen in summer or early autumn. As it is very sensitive to pollution, its numbers have recently decreased. It lives in groups of at most ten individuals and likes river estuaries, often swimming upstream short distances. It mainly feeds on fish of the sea floor and crustacea. Only in spring and autumn do Common Porpoises also hunt fish in the open ocean. They mate from June to October, and after a pregnancy of 10—11 months the female gives birth to a single young 60—85 cm long and weighing 3—8 kg. Recently, Common Porpoises have been caught for dolphinariums. They are extremely playful and manipulate objects not only by their mouth and anal fin, but very dextrously also by their flippers. The dorsal fin of cetaceans is not bony: it is formed by fatty and muscular tissue. Different species can be identified by the shape of the fin protruding above the surface (5, *Phocaena phocaena*; 6, *Orcinus orca*).

	L (m)	W
Orcinus orca	4.5—10	5—8 t
Pseudorca crassidens	2.5—5.5	1.2—1.7 t
Phocaena phocaena	1.5—1.8	30—60 kg

Index of Latin names

Acomys cahirinus 128
  dimidiatus 128
  russatus 128
Aethechinus algirus 40
Alces alces 148
Allactaga jaculus 140
Alopex lagopus 90
Ammotragus lervia 166
Apodemus agrarius 128
  flavicollis 126
  microps 126
  mystacinus 126
  sylvaticus 126
Arvicola sapidus 118
  terrestris 118

Balaena mysticetus 176
Balaenoptera borealis 172
  musculus 172
  physalus 172
Barbastella barbastellus 62
Bison bonasus 168
  bonasus 168
  caucasicus 168
Bubalus arnee 168
  f. bubalis 168

Canis aureus 88
  lupus 88
Capra aegagrus 162
  caucasica 164
  cylindricornis 164
  hircus 162
  ibex 164
  pyrenaica 164
Capreolus capreolus 152
Castor canadensis 110
  fiber 110
Cervus elaphus 156
  nippon 156
Citellus citellus 106
  pygmaeus 106
  suslicus 106
Clethrionomys glareolus 116
  rufocanus 116
  rutilus 116
Cricetulus migratorius 112
Cricetus cricetus 112
Crocidura leucodon 46
  russula 46
  suaveolens 46
Ctenodactylus gundi 144
Cystophora cristata 100

Dama dama 154
Delphinapterus leucas 178
Delphinus delphis 180
Desmana moschata 48
Dicrostonyx torquatus 114
Dryomys nitedula 138

Elephantulus roseti 48
Eliomys quercinus 138
Ellobius talpinus 124
Eptesicus nilssoni 58
  serotinus 58
Erignathus barbatus 98
Erinaceus concolor 40
  europaeus 40
Eubalaena glacialis 176
Eutamias sibiricus 108

Felis cattus 94
  lybica 94
  margarita 94
  ornata 94
  silvestris 94
Fennecus zerda 86

Galemys pyrenaicus 48
Gazella dorcas 158
  leptoceros 158
Genetta genetta 84
Glis glis 136
Globicephala melaena 180
Grampus griseus 180
Gulo gulo 76

Halichoerus gryphus 100
Hemiechinus auritus 40
Herpestes edwardsii 84
  ichneumon 84
Hyaena hyaena 86
Hydropotes inermis 152
Hystrix cristata 108

Jaculus jaculus 140

Kogia breviceps 174

Lagurus lagurus 116
Lemmus lemmus 114
  sibiricus 114
Lemniscomys barbarus 130
Lepus capensis 142
  europaeus 142
  timidus 142
Lutra lutra 78
Lutreola lutreola 68
  vison 68
Lycaon pictus 86
Lynx lynx 96
  pardina 96

Macaca sylvanus 64
Marmota bobac 104
  marmota 104
Martes foina 72
  cretica 72
  martes 72
  zibellina 72

Megaptera novaeangliae 174
Meles meles 74
Mesocricetus auratus 112
  raddei 112
Micromys minutus 130
Microtus agrestis 122
  arvalis 122
  guentheri 120
  nivalis 122
  oeconomus 122
Miniopterus schreibersi 62
Monachus monachus 100
Monodon monoceros 178
Muntiacus reevesi 152
Mus musculus 132
  domesticus 132
  musculus 132
  spicilegus 132
  spretus 132
Muscardinus avellanarius 136
Mustela erminea 66
  nivalis 66
  sibirica 66
Myocastor coypus 110
Myomimus roachi 138
Myopus schisticolor 114
Myotis brandti 54
  daubentoni 54
  myotis 54
  mystacinus 54

Neomys anomalus 44
  fodiens 44
Nyctalus lasiopterus 58
  leisleri 58
  noctula 58
Nyctereutes procyonoides 92

Odocoileus virginianus 154
Ondatra zibethicus 118
Orcinus orca 182
Oryctolagus cuniculus 144
Ovibos moschatus 170
  wardi 170
Ovis musimon 166
  orientalis 166

Pagophilus groenlandicus 98
Panthera pardus 96
Phoca vitulina 98
Phocaena phocaena 182
Pipistrellus kuhli 56
  nathusii 56
  pipistrellus 56
  savii 56

Physeter macrocephalus 174
Pitymyx duodecimostatus 120
  savii 120
  subterraneus 120
Plecotus auritus 60
  austriacus 60
Procyon lotor 92
Pseudorca crassidens 182
Pteromys volans 108
Pusa hispida 98
Putorius eversmanni 70
  putorius 70

Rangifer tarandus 150
Rattus norvegicus 134
  rattus 134
    alexandrinus 134
    frugivorus 134
    rattus 134
Rhinolophus blasii 52
  euryale 52
  ferrumequinum 52
  hipposideros 52
Rupicapra rupicapra 160

Saiga tatarica 158
Sciurus carolinensis 102
  vulgaris 102
Sicista betulina 140
  subtilis 140
Sorex alpinus 42
  araneus 42
  caecutiens 42
  minutissimus 42
  minutus 42
Spalax leucodon 124
  microphthalmus 124
Suncus etruscus 46
Sus scrofa 146

Tadarida teniotis 62
Talpa caeca 50
  europaea 50
  romana 50

Thalarctos maritimus 82
Tursiops truncatus 180

Ursus arctos 80
  syriacus 80

Vormela peregusna 70
Vulpes rüppelli 86
  vulpes 90

Index of common names

Aoudad 166
Ape, Barbary 64

Badger 74
Barbastelle 62
Bat, Blasius' Horseshoe 52
    Brandt's 54
    Daubenton's 54
    European Free-tailed 62
    Greater Horseshoe 52
    Grey Long-eared 60
    Giant Noctule 58
    Large Mouse-eared 54
    Leisler's 58
    Lesser Horseshoe 52
    Lesser Noctule 58
    Long-eared 60
    Mediterran Horseshoe 52
    Noctule 58
    Northern 58
    Schreiber's 62
    Serotine 58
    Water 54
    Whiskered 54
    see also Pipistrelle
Beaver, Canadian 110
    European 110
Bear, Brown 80
    Polar 82
    Syrian 80
Beluga 178
Bison, European 168
Boar, Wild 146
Buffalo, Indian 168
    Water 168

Carabao 168
Cat, African Wild 94
    European Wild 94
    Sand 94
    Steppe 94
Chamois 160
Chipmunk, Siberian 108
Coypu 110

Deer, Chinese Water 152
    Fallow 154
    Red 156
    Roe 152
    Sika 156
    Virginian 154
    White-tailed 154
Desman, Pyrenean 48
    Russian 48
Dog, African Hunting 86
Dolphin, Bottlenosed 180
    Common 180
    Risso's 180
Dormouse, British 136
    Common 136

Edible 136
Fat 136
Forest 138
Garden 138
Hazel 136
Mouse-like 138
Oak 138
Ognev's 138
Squirrel-tailed 136

Elk 148
Ermine 66
Eutamias 108

Fennec 86
Fox, Arctic 90
    Red 90
    Sand 86

Gazelle, Dorcas 158
    Slender-horned 158
Genet, European 84
    Feline 84
    Small-spotted 84
Glutton 76
Goat, Domestic 162
    Wild 162
Gundi 144

Hamster, Common 112
    Golden 112
    Grey 112
    Migratory 112
    Radde's Golden 112
Hare, African 142
    Arctic 142
    Blue 142
    Brown 142
    Common 142
    European 142
    Mountain 142
Hedgehog, Algerian 40
    Eastern 40
    European 40
    Long-eared 40
    Vagrant 40
Hyena, Laughing 86
    Painted 86
    Striped 86

Ibex 164
    Caucasian 164
    Daghestan 164
    Pyrenean 164
Ichneumon 84

Jackal, Golden 88
    Indian 88
Jerboa, Desert 140
    Five-toed 140

Killer, False 182

Lemming, Collared 114
    Mole 124
    Norway 114
    Siberian 114
    Wood 114
Leopard 96
Lynx 96
    Northern 96
    Spanish 96

Marmot, Alpine 104
    Bobac 104
Marten, Beech 72
    Pine 72
    Stone 72
Mink, American 68
    European 68
Mole, Blind 50
    Common 50
    Mediterranean 50
    Roman 50
Mole Rat, Greater 124
    Lesser 124
    Russian 124
Mongoose, Egyptian 84
    Indian 84
Moose 148
Mouflon 166
Mouse, Algerian House 132
    Broad-toothed Field 126
    Cairo Spiny 128
    Egyptian Spiny 128
    Golden Spiny 128
    Harvest 130
    House 132
    Long-tailed Field 126
    Northern Birch 140
    Pygmy Wood 126
    Rock 126
    Southern Birch 140
    Striped Field 128
    Striped Grass 130
    Wood 126
    Yellow-necked 126
Muntjac, Chinese 152
    Reeve's 152
Musk-ox 170
Muskrat 110

Narwhal 178
Noctule, Common 58
    Giant 58
    Lesser 58
Nutria 110

Otter 78

Panther 96
Pardel 96
Pipistrelle, Common 56
    Kuhl's 56
    Nathusius' 56

Savi's 56
Polecat, Asiatic 70
    European 70
    Marbled 70
    Steppe 70
Porcupine, Common 108
    Crested 108
Porpoise, Common 182

Rabbit 144
Raccoon 92
Raccoon Dog 92
Rat, Black 134
    Brown 134
    Jumping 140
    Norwegian 134
    Ship 134
Reindeer 150
Rorqual, Common 172

Sable 72
Saiga 158
Seal, Atlantic 100
    Bearded 98
    Common 98
    Grey 100
    Harbour 98
    Harp 98
    Hooded 100
    Monk 100
    Ringed 98
Sheep, Barbary 166
Shrew, Alpine 42
    Bicoloured White-toothed 46
    Common 42
    Common European White-toothed 46
    Etruscan 46
    Laxmann's 42
    Least 42
    Lesser White-toothed 46
    Masked 42
    Mediterranean Water 44
    North-African Elephant 48
    Pygmy 42
    Savi's Pygmy 46
    Scilly 46
    Water 44
Souslik, European 106
    Pygmy 106
    Spotted 106
Squirrel, Flying 108
    Grey 102
    Ground 106
    Red 102
    Russian Flying 108
Stoat 66

Tolai 142

Vole, Alpine 122
    Bank 116
    Dwarf Fruit-eating 118
    European Pine 120
    Field 122

Grey-sided 116
Guenther's 120
Iberian Root 120
Large-toothed Red-backed 116
Mediterranean 120
Mediterranean Pine 120
Mediterranean Root 120
Northern 116
Ruddy Red-backed 116
Sagebrush 116
Savi's Pine 120
Short-tailed 122
Snow 122
Tundra 122
Water 118

Weasel 66

Siberian 66
Whale, Biscayan 176
Blue 172
False Killer 182
Fin 172
Greenland Right 176
Humpback 174
Killer 182
North Atlantic Right 176
Pilot 180
Pygmy Sperm 174
Sei 172
Sperm 174
White 178
Wisent 168
Wolf 88
Wolverine 76

Bibliography

M. BOUCHNER, 1982. *Animal tracks and traces.* Octopus, London.

F. H. van den BRINK, 1975. *Die Säugetiere Europas.* Paul Parey Verl., Hamburg u. Berlin.

M. BURTON, 1971. *The Observer's Book of Wild Animals.* Frederick Warne, London and New York.

G. CORBET and D. OVENDEN, 1980. *The Mammals of Britain and Europe.* Collins, London.

J. DORST and P. DANDELOT, 1970. *A Field Guide to the Larger Mammals of Africa.* Collins, London.

J. R. ELLERMANN and T. C. S. MORRISON-SCOTT, 1951. *Checklist of Palaearctic and Indian Mammals.* British Museum (N. H.), London.

V. E. FLINT, J. D. CHOGUNOV and V. M. SMIRIN, 1970. *Mlekopitayushchie.* Moscow.

J. E. KING, 1964. *Seals of the World.* British Museum (N. H.), London.

E. MOHR, 1950. *Die freilebenden Nagetiere Deutschlands.* Jena.

E. MOHR, 1952. *Die Robben der europäischen Gewässer. Monografie der Säugetiere.* Frankfurt/Main.

H. PETZSCH, 1963. *Die Katzen.* Urania Verl., Leipzig—Jena—Berlin.